PRAISE FOR
Rudy's Rules for Travel

"As often as Rudy's rules caused trouble for his anxiety-riddled wife, they also led to astonishing moments of wonder, especially at the kindness and generosity of strangers. . . . From exotic destinations like Bali to more personal excursions to uncover family history, Rudy's travels are imbued with his unceasing optimism and boundless enthusiasm, leaving the reader convinced that his rules are well worth following."

—*Booklist*

"This intelligent and entertaining memoir has fun with the lifetime perambulations of Mary and her late husband, a World War II airman who had faced the terror of death on an almost daily basis, and survived. Rudy came out of this character-shaping experience with both a zest for living and a fearless attitude. Their travels followed Rudy's rules, the most important of which was—to trust in the kindness of strangers. This memoir is an insightful record of human interactions and a hilarious account of their journeys, with a laugh on almost every page."

—Charles B. Churchill, PhD, historian and author of
Adventurers and Prophets and *Through the Needle's Eye:
Elite Rule and the Illusions of Freedom*

"Mary K. Jensen's delightful writing hooks you into each chapter, making you laugh out loud at her observations and humor. I would have liked to spend my vacations with these two travelers, but I am glad I could at least take these journeys through her writings."

—Cathy Chase, author of *JUMP*

"Among the reasons people ride on roller coasters are to experience thrills and surprise and test personal boundaries, but, unlike traveling independently overseas, roller coasters are basically predictable. Mary K. Jensen, while crafting warm, vivid pictures of the places she and her fearless husband, Rudy, visited, makes it possible for us to feel what it is like to be pulled along, always wondering what's coming next on trips to new destinations. While rewarding readers with insights gained from the encounters that she and Rudy had, this book inspires stepping into the unknown."

—David Tykol, Editor, *International Travel News*, Sacramento, CA

Rudy's Rules for Travel

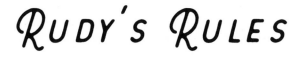

Rudy's Rules

for

Travel

LIFE LESSONS FROM
AROUND THE GLOBE

By

Mary K. Jensen

SHE WRITES PRESS

Published 2018
Printed in the United States of America
print: 978-1-63152-322-9
ebook: 978-1-63152-323-6
LCCN: 2017955000

For information, address:
She Writes Press
1563 Solano Ave #546
Berkeley, CA 94707

She Writes Press is a division of SparkPoint Studio, LLC.

"The kindness of strangers" reference: from *A Streetcar Named Desire,* Tennessee Williams, 1947.

Certain descriptions and dialogue are based on *Tales and Memories,* Rudolf S. Jensen, 1999.

"Life is not a journey to the grave...." Reprinted with permission of Mark Frost, *The Match: The Day the Game of Golf Changed Forever.* 2007. Good Comma Ink, Inc.

"An Old Man" reprinted with permission of author Robert Pinsky, *Robert Pinsky Selected Poems. 2011.* Farrar, Straus and Giroux.

All photos not taken by the author are credited to Shutterstock.

Although this is a true story, some names and identifying details have been changed to protect individual privacy.

Book design by Stacey Aaronson

To Rudy

COMING TO AMERICA

Table of Contents

Rudy's Rules

Travel

Chapter One

Rudy's Rules for Travel

MOST HONEYMOONS DO NOT START THIS WAY.

I tell myself there are good reasons why I have crawled out the attic window at midnight and am now lying outside on the sloping roof in Edinburgh dressed in a light cotton nightgown, somewhat secured by a bed sheet strung round my waist and tied to a handy balustrade. It is, after all, a record-smashing heat wave in the Scottish capital. Hotels and air conditioning are not in our budget, and all non-attic bed and breakfast rooms were reserved weeks ago. By others.

I know all that, but I also know that the real reason I am on the roof, clutching my pillow and my groom, is because of one of Rudy's Rules for Travel, perhaps the most significant one of all. Rule One: Adapt.

BEFORE that scorching summer of 1980, Rudy and I had traveled together several times. (Notice I say "traveled" and not "vacationed." There is a reason for that.) I had learned that he had many rules, and that some were easier to follow than others. Following the rule about choosing lightweight luggage was, for example, easier than following the rule about adapting.

RUDY knew a lot about rule making: he had been raised in a German home and was a school principal nine months of the year. Each school holiday, in a transformation not unlike that of Clark Kent to Superman, he exchanged suit and tie for battered jeans, faded navy captain's hat, plaid shirt, and back-pack, leaving razor and dress shoes scattered behind. Even his eyes changed: in the school year, the deep blue eyes could be narrow and fixed unwaveringly, sternly, on sixth-grade boys who would destroy classroom peace. But when ready for travel, the blue eyes danced.

My fearless half was made for adventure travel—not the climb-Everest kind of adventure, but the can-you-make-your-own-way adventure. In fact, in the late twentieth century, when we traveled, you did not need to dive, climb, or kayak to feel a surge of explorer's adrenalin. When a traveler descended the steps from the airplane and walked onto a foreign tarmac, it was without online reservations, GPS, Google maps, ATM cards, translation apps, Uber, Skype, or Trip Advisor. There was no CNN, nor were there online state department bulletins to warn of global hotspots.

Most importantly, yesterday's traveler ventured without a cell phone. When you were lost, you were lost alone. This was not entirely a disadvantage: no demanding boss could find an escaping worker, and news of tragedies across the world was kept at bay, restricted to the daily English newspaper—if and only if the traveler chose to read it.

In those years, contact with home meant writing post-cards that, with luck and first-class postage, arrived two weeks later. Or it meant spending hours in a local phone booth pleading with an operator who insisted, in perfect English, she did not speak English. One was simply "abroad."

RUDY and I were a picture of contrast. He was tall, thin, far-sighted, confident—an artist and scholar. I was not. Not any of that. We were of different generations and mind-sets. As I was being born, Rudy was flying one of his first bombing missions over Germany. As my parents were pushing my stroller in a Victory Day parade, he was in the middle of the Atlantic, coming home in a troop ship with his wounded comrades. And as I was walking to kindergarten clutching my nap-time blanket, he was one of those GIs who had never dreamed of college yet stood smiling in cap and gown. For him, travel was a way to piece together the parts of his life. For me, travel was a way to make the storybook pictures come alive.

Most significantly, my new husband and I lived at opposite ends of the risk-taking continuum. Imagine a horizontal bar, if you will. On its far left is the ultimate risk-taker, and on the far right the ultimate worrier. I am the one clinging to the bar on the far right, while Rudy is dancing on the left edge. You get the picture.

A similar continuum shows our typical thought patterns. While I pondered my latest catastrophic awareness, Rudy could take a spontaneous leap straight off the edge. Put in neurological terms, I had an overly developed frontal lobe and he a damaged impulse-control center. Put in astrological terms, I was a Libra, he a Taurus. When we met, I was a newly hired psychologist in his school district. Before long, he was explaining to friends that we were ideally matched: I needed an administrator; he needed a psychologist.

Many of our differences can be traced to the brown chair that sat near the front door of my childhood home. Under the surveillance of our half-Irish mother, the chair governed the comings and goings of my younger brother Donnie and me. We could be racing through the house, grabbing textbooks and snacks, catapulting toward the front door, but we were captives until we had each placed our bottom in the chair and taken three deep breaths, 1 . . . 2 . . . 3 . . . . Forgetting a homework assignment or lunch pail restarted the cycle:

racing back into the house, mother watching for bottom to hit chair, then chest heave three times before the race to school could resume.

"You'll see the good luck," Mom would call after us. "Stay composed."

Rudy had never sat down to gain composure. He had, instead, an ease with exploration that came naturally and at a young age. By age four, he completed two transatlantic crossings, the first in 1921 while carried in the womb of his mother from New York City to Hamburg, Germany. His papa, a Danish seaman, was an admirer of German culture who harbored two dreams: one, that he would father a German citizen and two, that he would own a saloon on Hamburg's lively Reeperbahn. Achieving the dreams meant nothing when his wife, Rudy's mother, died suddenly. Papa found foster care for the toddler and headed back to sea. Years later, he sent for Rudy to join him in America.

And so it was that the four-year-old experienced his first independent international travel. Dressed in a tiny sailor suit, blonde curls escaping a captain's hat, blue eyes gleaming, and trained to salute the ship's officers, Rudy crossed the Atlantic for the second time, but now virtually alone. He learned a lifelong travel lesson about depending upon kind strangers: two elderly ladies shared their cabin and mealtimes with him, and the captain helped him sail bright red balloons off the ship's stern. Sailing into New York Harbor, the little boy spotted his papa on the dock and was certain he called his name.

Rudy grew up on the streets of Washington, D.C. during the Great Depression. He and his schoolmates, from Italy and Greece, found ample adult role models: Chisel Chin the cop, Fast Eddie the numbers runner, Horse Face the cabbie and card room dealer. I never knew the Depression or the streets. I came home after school to a small, bungalow-style house in Southern California where a mother in a pink-flowered apron was placing a plate of warm chocolate chip cookies on the kitchen table.

Rudy's family never owned a car, but instead used every form of bus and train that plied the city. The highlight of humid summer weekends was dragging heavy crab traps onto a small steam train, heading to Chesapeake Bay, and bringing home—yes, on the train—a week's worth of feisty critters housed unhappily in burlap bags. Rudy had had, we might say, the perfect introduction to public transportation around the world.

I, on the other hand, was driven to school each morning in my father's well-used but shiny, cavernous black-and-white Cadillac. Donnie and I sat in the backseat, dodging ice chips that flew from the air conditioning vents, until Father rounded the corner in front of our school. Then we slid down between the seats, covering our heads with jackets, lest classmates who knew how to use the public bus should see us in the Cadillac.

"Please, please drop us at the next block," we pled from under the jackets.

Our father was not a seaman or world traveler; our father was an accountant. Each spring, Donnie and I counted the days to April 15th, when tax season would end and we could embark on our annual family adventure. The ritual began with stuffing the Cadillac with seashore clothes, a sand pail, and food supplies, then taking a careful look at a large map and setting off. Twenty-five minutes later we would arrive at our destination: a local beach-area motel. We would then unpack our clothes, pail, and food, and settle in for a three-day stay.

As our parents saw it, the glorious part of the holiday was that there was no long drive from home, no telephone, and no way clients could find Father. As I saw it, the annual outing was a rare opportunity to gather material for fourth grade Show and Tell. Surprisingly one day, Donnie, barely five years old, was the source of key intelligence: an older boy he met at the sandcastle pointed with concern to an island, a distant landmass barely visible across the bay. As children of the Cold War, we knew how to duck and cover under classroom desks. Still, it never occurred to me before that day that there might be a wider, threatening world out there, just beyond San Diego. I was learning the lesson that you can never be too cautious. Donnie and I were certain Russia lurked on the island.

NOW, on this steamy night in Edinburgh so many years later, Rudy, my groom, arms draped about me, snores softly on the sloping roof. I stay awake, for I have rules of my own: "Remain Alert. Expect the worst." Scotland may not be known for earthquakes or monsoons, but one can never be too careful.

Rudy's Rules
for
Travel

1. **ADAPT.**

2. **RUN CROSSCURRENT.**
   Avoid groups. Schedule your own tour. Shower at night, keep drapes open, rise with first light. Be first at breakfast. At the museum, start at the last exhibit and move forward.

3. **GO IN DISGUISE OR, MINIMALLY, KEEP A LOW PROFILE.**
   Accept that Americans are not always popular. Study natives' clothing, haircuts, shoes; outfit yourself at a secondhand store. Speak any language but English if you can; at the least, lower voices when dining and on public transit.

4. **NEVER LET LUGGAGE HOLD YOU BACK.**
   Use one small, child-sized case or backpack. Prepare to run unimpeded through airports and stations, up stairs, over cobblestones.
   Which is closely related to this rule:

5. **NEVER SHOWER ALONE.**
   Position the day's dirty clothes under your feet, add soap, stomp, as in crushing grapes.

6. **RIDE WITH LOCALS, NOT TOURISTS.**
   A low-cost way to meet the people and their livestock: ride their buses, vans, ferries, colectivos, tuk-tuks.

7. **LOOK FOR THE FREE LUNCH: YOU NEED TO SAVE FOR THE NEXT TRIP.**

   You don't get what you pay for if you miss bargains. Exception: elephant rides (see Thailand chapter).

8. **AVOID RECOMMENDED RESTAURANTS.**
   They will be crowded, pricey, and the food likely mediocre. Choose cafés off the main square, with no tour bus or English menus in sight. Better yet, bring deli food to your room.

9. **YOU CAN'T GO HOME AGAIN.**
   Never visit the same place twice; there are too many places. Returning risks spoiling first memories.

10. **SELECT SOUVENIRS BY WEIGHT AND VOLUME.**
    Recommended: earrings, miniature Christmas ornaments.

11. **RELAX. SOME KIND STRANGER WILL APPEAR.**

12. **PUT THE BUCKET IN ORDER.**
    Don't count on tomorrow. You will likely never be healthier than you are today. You certainly will never be younger. Move physically challenging destinations to the top of your bucket list. (Think: climbing pyramids, squatting over toilets, mounting steep stairs without handrails.) Consider moving politically tenuous places higher: there may be no better days ahead. Cruises can wait.

13. **NEVER COME HOME WITHOUT HAVING PLANNED THE NEXT TRIP.**
    That is what all those hours on the return plane are for.

CHAPTER TWO

MEXICO CITY
1976
MEXICO

IT IS LONG BEFORE ONLINE RESEARCH AND EXPEDIA WHEN Rudy and I plan our first trip together. I have an early sign that the journey to Mexico City might not be the luxurious vacation of my dreams, when Rudy appears at my apartment door with a tiny case, a gift for me.

"I remembered your luggage was huge. This one will go anywhere."

"But that's a child's suitcase."

"Exactly."

"But at most it holds one set of clothes."

"Exactly."

Reaching an impasse on luggage, we turn instead to sharing results of our research for the trip. Each of us has promised to gather information. I have gone to a travel agency; Rudy has gone to the library. I come to the table with five slick tour brochures carefully annotated for their positive features, likely omissions, and daily cost. He presents a map and three thick books, one that promises the reader will be bilingual in Spanish in thirty days, one detailing Mexican history, and one that introduces techniques for archeological digs.

I venture to summarize what I see. "So, we don't take a tour? We're our own guides?"

"Well, yes. We call the airlines and get the cheapest flight."

"And book a hotel?"

"Well, if you want one for the first night."

"For the first night? And after that?"

"We look around. We don't travel to have comfort . . . we can have comfort at home. And we don't travel to meet Americans. We can meet Americans at home. Besides, hotel prices are cheaper on-site."

That was putting it mildly. Arriving at the Mexico City airport, we spot a crowd of travelers huddling around a newspaper stand. The English-language newspaper has a full banner headline: "Peso Drastically Devalued." A fellow tourist explains that our dollar has just skyrocketed in Mexico; any hotel of our dreams is within reach.

Clearly the hostel-like lodging we reserved can be replaced, but there are other ways to save a peso. Rudy recalls reading about the *colectivo* taxis. Consulting his portable Spanish dictionary, and with some linguistic help from two porters and one policeman, he selects a weathered *colectivo* already packed with three other tourists ("Think of how cheap this will be"), jams our cases into the trunk ("See why we pack small?"), and asks the driver to take us to a "*muy bueno*" hotel.

"A very *muy bueno* hotel."

This is the fastest taxi ride I have ever experienced and surely with the most sincere of tour guides. While I am in the backseat, trying to ascertain which passenger lap I should land on, Rudy sits in front with the driver, rolls down his window, and all along the route points out key monuments and their historic significance. The driver, enthused by Rudy's interest, gestures proudly to highlights of his own, barely bothering to hold the steering wheel or note the traffic swirling around us. Our fellow passengers are mute. As we pull up to the luxurious hotel beside the entrance to Chapultepec Park, I say a short prayer of thanks and Rudy turns to me, grinning. "Isn't it lucky I'm bilingual?"

That night we take a long walk through the elegant neighborhood of our *muy bueno* hotel. Massive strands of Christmas lights are strung across each intersection, like multiple jeweled necklaces. Either a life-size nativity scene or a live Santa Claus sits on every corner, backdrops for annual pictures of children dressed in lacy holiday finery.

Shortly, I become distracted from the holiday traditions. "Look, look at those store windows—Cartier and Gucci are slashing prices."

Rudy is uninterested. Looking in all directions, he says, "There ought to be street stands around here somewhere. You cannot believe the bargains I've gotten in Tijuana and Juarez."

I persist: "And over there, there's Burberry and Bulgari. The big designers are all here. With the peso devalued, those prices are a third of what we'd pay in the States."

He also persists: "You have to get off the main shopping drag to find the real Mexican clothes."

Luxury stores don't attract Rudy. He has eyes only for street merchants and their wares, hungry for the bargain. After one very long, dramatic exchange in which Rudy uses his best Spanish to negotiate a *serape* for me and *huaraches* for himself, I hear the merchant ask his companion, in English, "What language was that man speaking, anyway?"

The next morning, after checking to be certain that breakfast is included in our room rate, Rudy invites me to eat in the opulent dining room. I have never before had breakfast served on fine china and under chandeliers, with tuxedoed waiters hovering and my fellow diners looking as if *they* had not passed up the luxury stores last night.

Rudy's linguistic skills get us through a quick menu reading, and plates of *huevos rancheros* arrive successfully. Emboldened, Rudy—in his Spanish—asks the waiter where he can find the men's room. The waiter hesitates, looking puzzled before he says, "*En el parque ... en Chapultepec.*" A few more rounds ensue of Rudy and the waiter both looking confused and repeating the Q and A, with the waiter finally pointing out the large window toward the adjacent park. In an attempt to be even more explicit, he bobs up and down with both fists closed and says something close to "giddyup."

This waiter looks for all the world like someone riding a horse.

Rudy's blue eyes open even wider than usual. He furtively consults his Spanish dictionary: "Horse! *Caballo*! Say, that could sound like *caballeros*. Maybe I haven't perfected my accent yet."

As he returns from the *caballeros*, the men's room, located quite conveniently in the restaurant, he encounters the smiling faces of the other waiters as they all bob up and down, fists closed, as in a horse race.

✈

WE fill our days with excursions on local buses or in the *colectivos* to museums, galleries, the park, and the Zocala. Rudy insists on capping off each day's touring with a leisurely ride on a local bus, returning home with the tired workers of the city. The strategy is simple: choose a different bus each afternoon to discover neighborhoods no tour group would find, ride to the end of its line, then stay on the bus and ride back to the city with the driver. Lesson learned: make sure it is not the very last route of the day. The last route of the day ends in a dark, deserted bus yard twenty miles from the city center.

In the evenings, we stroll with families in the colorful squares, listening to mariachis and admiring young ones' dress clothes and shiny new patent shoes. In each place, Rudy's advance work helps us find the treasures we know await us, like the Diego Rivera murals, as well as the treasures we do not know are waiting, like the tiny boy who sits for hours cross-legged on the floor of the Museo de Anthropologica, sketching the diorama that commemorates his country's War of Independence.

We have one more sight on our touring list—the grand Pyramids outside the city. They are a distance away and time is running short, so Rudy compromises his rules and agrees with me that we should join a daylong group tour. Good thing we did. How else could we have found the souvenir shop run by our guide's second cousin by marriage, or the beer-drinking burro out back of the Pyramids? (Note to the curious: the burro approaches a standing, open bottle of Dos Equis, grasps it in his mouth, throws back his head, and gulps.) It's memorable.

At the end of the week, when it is time for us to leave the hotel, we pay a shockingly low bill at the hotel desk, then turn and make our way toward the front door. Some members of the restaurant staff stand on either side of the doorway, forming a kind of honor guard before they break into grins, close their fists, bob up and down, and say *adios* to their *amigo*, their *buen amigo*.

Chapter Three

OAXACA
1979
MEXICO

I AM A RELUCTANT LEARNER, BUT I AM LEARNING. FOR example, public buses can lead to the public's treasures. We spend the week before Easter in Oaxaca, a magnificent colonial city in the center of Mexico, staying in a hacienda-style inn high in the hills above the main square.

I have done research at the hotel desk and summarize for Rudy:

"There are two ways to get down to the Zocala, the main plaza. There's one taxi that's recommended, and really reasonable, and one taxi that's not so recommended and a little cheaper. Really, they are almost the same price and you can guess which is truly the better deal."

"Sure, I can guess . . . right out front there's a bus stop."

Our fellow passengers smile or nod as we board the battered bus, making room for us to sit amongst woven bags of produce and crates of poultry. I position myself between lettuce and potatoes, carefully avoiding beaks of roosters that protrude from crates at my feet. Rudy starts a mostly hand-gestures conversation with the people around him.

"Want restaurant, *authéntico* restaurant." And emphatically: "No *turista*."

I add an idea, "*Turista* okay, enchiladas *buenos*."

Rudy clarifies, "*Muy authéntico restaurant, buenos* enchiladas."

Ideas abound and disagreements ensue as our companions argue for their favorite places, some owned by cousins, some not. At last there is a consensus and one of the men gestures to me that he needs a pen and paper. He draws a map, carefully depicting the bus, the bus stop in the square, and small feet leading in a path to our *authéntico* restaurant.

Thirty minutes later we get off the coughing bus right at town center, returning the waves of our fellow passengers and brushing a few chicken feathers from our coats. We begin following the little map, but before we have gone more than a few steps, I look up and spot two elegant restaurants perched above the beautiful colonial square, each with a romantic wrought-iron balcony covered with mounds and mounds of purple and red bougainvillea. I am sure I hear soft guitars in the background and smell *buenos* enchiladas being cooked for me.

"Look at those restaurants, Rude—what wonderful views of the churches and plaza." I don't mention the tour buses I see parked along the side streets, or the fact that four out of five patrons going in the front door have an American guide-book tucked under their arms.

"But the map shows *authéntico* just blocks away, and we have evaluation criteria for restaurants. We've agreed on those," Rudy says.

It is true we have agreed on the evaluation checklist, but that was before I saw the bougainvillea.

Footsteps on the map lead to the recommended *taquería*. The small, simple restaurant clearly meets criteria: a crowded local favorite, at least two blocks off town center, Spanish menus only, no view, no tour buses or American guidebooks in sight.

We take the last seats available at a long table. It is a fine dinner—*buenos* enchiladas for me, *carnitas* tacos for Rudy. He beams, as the *cerveza* is the cheapest he has ever drunk and the communal table is giving him a chance to practice his bilingual skills. For the most part that is going well. As time goes on, there are fewer and fewer puzzled looks as either Rudy's Spanish or the *cerveza* improves.

We finish our meal about the same time as the other diners, noticing that the restaurant is gradually getting quiet. Conversations that earlier had been lively and high-pitched are now subdued, nearly still. Then almost as one, the diners begin to rise in silence from their tables, going to the door in what looks like a kind of procession. It is, we remember now, Holy Thursday, and we find ourselves welcomed by our tablemates to join them. We hesitate. We are not in Oaxaca for religious services. We are here because our school vacation is this week. We are, in short, imposters.

But there is no refusing the sincerity of our new friends, so we add to a stream of what becomes hundreds of the faithful, moving toward the plaza, lighting candles against the full-moon night, humming hymns of familiar melody if not words. We progress from the cathedral to smaller churches, moving up the central aisle of each, falling to our knees for a few moments, rising, lighting small vigil candles, and moving on to the next sanctuary.

Once in the midst of the fervent crowd, it is physically and emotionally impossible for us to leave until the last of seven churches has been visited and the pilgrimage dissolves. When that time comes, some hours having passed, we arrive back in the plaza. I look up to see tourists in the two restaurants above us leaning out over the balconies. They are straining to see, to understand what has happened on the streets below. I see what they had missed. They had missed the bus.

Chapter Four

PUERTO ESCONDIDO
1979
MEXICO

I AM LOOKING INTO THE EYES OF A GOAT. THE ANIMAL
stands high upon the tall rocky mountain, between even taller
trees, staring at the little airplane struggling through the narrow passage. I am in that plane.

There is a lesson to be learned here: ask Rudy for more
detail when he says, "This route is famous for spectacular,
once-in-a-lifetime scenery."

I could have stayed a good portion of my lifetime in colonial Oaxaca. We take day trips with friendly drivers to Zapotec heritage sites, Mitla, Monte Alban, and Indian markets. On Good Friday, we stand in the Zocala watching the slow, perfectly soundless procession, men laboring under heavy crosses through the streets. On Easter Sunday, we watch the square transform into a joyous parade ground of children in starched dresses and suits, their laughter mixing with a chorus of church bells ringing across the city.

But I note the restlessness growing in Rudy. He is prowling brochure stands and windows of travel agencies, scanning for information about the coast that lies nearly two hundred miles away. Judging from what he reads, the small town Puerto Escondido offers the perfect combination of beautiful scenery, low prices, and few if any tourists. He has heard the siren call familiar to all frugal explorers and is ready to move on.

"Nobody recommends we drive ourselves through the mountain range, but there's a bus and a plane to Puerto Escondido," he says. "I've talked to a lot of people and it sounds like the bus may not be so good. It takes eight or nine hours and the roads are mostly one-way, winding and steep. But they do say the drivers honk on blind curves . . ."

I vote for the plane ride, trusting that if not safer it would at least be over sooner. Rudy could not be more pleased, and that alarms me. We will fly in a vintage World War II craft.

"What an honor, honey, to ride in the DC-3. That plane was our workhorse in the war. We owe it so much."

We are unable to get reservations for the mid-morning

flight, but apparently that is not because the flight is so popular. "Just be there," the hotel clerk tells us, "and see if it goes today."

At the strip of land that has been designated the city airport, a veteran plane sits in a tin-roofed hangar. It does not look as if it will be going far today: engine parts are scattered on the ground all around the vintage craft, and two workers are deep in consultation.

"It looks like today is maintenance day," Rudy says.

"Well, yes. I bet most days are."

As we pick up our suitcases and search for a ride to the bus station, one of the engine repairmen shows us a second, very small plane, just a little larger than a crop duster. I have been blessed in multiple churches and lit votive lights throughout the town this Holy Week. I should be prepared for this flight, but my faith is challenged when my seat in the second row with the suitcases has a temperamental seat belt.

Before takeoff, the little plane roars and roars as it taxies past the mute DC-3. There is some kind of coming-of-age ritual going on here between these two. But after the roars, it sputters.

"Nothing to worry about," Rudy says. "Oaxaca is at 5,000 feet and it's hard for any plane to lift off from here."

Small comfort. We rise slowly, very slowly, with every part of our craft rattling or groaning, beginning a flight that will take us at tree and goat level through narrow, rugged passages of the Sierra del Sur mountain range to the coast. I am thrown about in my small space, hanging on to the window frame and suitcase beside me. Breathe in, 1 . . . exhale . . . 2 . . . inhale . . . 3 . . .

Now if I can just make myself open my eyes, I might see that spectacular, once-in-a-lifetime scenery. But when I do pry one eye open, I see large metal parts in a canyon below. Clearly remnants of the early-morning flight. There is no use attempting to share my innermost thoughts with Rudy; the engine noise covers any communication.

Miraculously, after two long hours, our little plane bounces into Puerto Escondido, coming to rest on an unpaved strip of land.

There is a second lesson to be learned from this trip: beware of tourist brochures that have wet ink and make promises such as, "You can be first to discover this paradise," or "Enjoy a hidden fishing village," or "Share the secrets of surfers."

A worker at the landing offers us a ride to the hotel Rudy has reserved, but when we reach the rather remote address, our driver scratches his head in confusion, looks again at the reservation form, then shrugs his shoulders and lifts our suitcases up to the porch of a seaside bungalow. Our gracious hostess gestures for us to sit in petite rattan chairs while she fetches us soft drinks, then points out two hammocks that line either side of the porch before beckoning us to follow her down a short hallway. Once inside, she shows us a small, obviously shared bathroom, then turns and takes us back to the porch.

In his unique mix of languages, Rudy asks her to show us our room and our bed. It is her turn to now look puzzled, as she points again to the two hammocks with woolen blankets and mosquito nets adorning them. A lot of understanding passes wordlessly between Rudy and me—it is growing late and dark, we are exhausted enough to sleep anywhere, and we have no car. We will find something else in the morning, but in the meantime, we need two pillows.

I do not usually spend time in a hammock and am unprepared for how responsive it is to movement. My every toss or turn tumbles me out, landing me on the mat below. About halfway through the long night, I decide to stay on the mat and entertain myself until sunrise with the sounds of birds, insects, and Rudy's snoring.

The birds get louder, and at the very first glimmer of day I waken Rudy. Just as at home, he insists he has not had a moment of sleep all night and that he has not snored. We walk toward town, searching for breakfast, a bed, and a room. Fishermen are already dragging small boats up to the crescent-shaped shore, untangling brightly colored nets and holding aloft the catches of the day. The village is quiet and beautiful, just as advertised. We are beginning to think the port might be too authentic, too lacking in traveler comforts, when like a mirage we spot a few tourists at the end of the crescent shore, eating bountiful breakfasts in a beachfront, open-air, colorfully tiled restaurant. Our path runs in front of the diners, close enough that we can see onto their plates. Rudy spots an entire grilled red snapper hanging off the sides of one earthenware platter.

"*Huachinango,* that guy has a whole *huachinango,*" he says, picking up his pace and heading into the restaurant. "I bet it came right out of a fisherman's net this morning."

Our waitress Alicia knows enough English to assure Rudy his personal *huachinango* was netted within the hour and, better yet, the restaurant is part of a small hotel. Her husband Carlos will drive us back to our hammocks to retrieve luggage; room 15, complete with a bed, is ours. Rudy barely looks at the charming room.

"I love being close to fish," he says.

That night Alicia tells us our timing is *muy bueno*. We are here for the first night, the grand opening, of her nephew's restaurant and bar. There will be mariachis and margaritas and the finest food outside of Restaurant Santa Fe.

"Don't leave for there early," Alicia advises. "Wait for the party to start."

It is nine o'clock when we follow the balloon-lined street and the sound of mariachis. Two traditionally costumed children, a boy and girl seven or perhaps eight years old, stand outside the freshly painted white restaurant, handing us flyers announcing the big night. As we enter, the children smile broadly and nod to each other, then take us by the hand and lead us to a large round table dressed in a starched white cloth and bountiful floral bouquet.

Before the mariachis can begin their next number, three young waiters in tuxedos surround us. One offers us a margaritas menu, another a list of food of the day, and the third watches the first two. We are the only diners in the large decorated room, and for the rest of the night the three men stand behind us, watching with great studiousness as each bite of tamale and enchilada enters our mouths, looking at us quizzically and asking after every taste, "*Bueno?*" or "*Muy bueno?*" Periodically, the children and mariachis ring our table, joining the waiters in their study of our digestive processes. At one point I look for a restroom. Two older women in aprons come from the kitchen to escort me, then they wait outside the door for me to emerge. "*Bueno?*" they ask. I have to assume they are inquiring about the colorful bathroom décor and the new toilet. I say, "*Muy bueno.*"

We feel the pain of a limited Spanish vocabulary, for the evening is far beyond *bueno* or even *muy bueno.* We have to settle in the end for handshakes and "*adios*" until tomorrow.

CHAPTER FIVE

WEST 1980 GERMANY

"WOULD YOU RATHER EAT AT THE COFFEE SHOP DOWN THE
street or have croissants at a sidewalk café in Paris?" At
home, Rudy will ask the same question for twenty years.

I will have the same answer for twenty years: "Forced to a
choice, it's croissants."

For nine months each year, we save all possible dollars at
home so that in June, in some foreign bank, they might
transform into confusing coins and colorful bills.

✈

THIS spring is unusually busy for me at work, and I relinquish summer trip planning to Rudy. I learn never to do this again.

"But you know how I hate details," he says.

"Yes, but this time we're in your land, your Germany."

"That's the problem."

"That's the problem—that you're in your homeland?" I ask the question before I can stop myself. I know the answer well, and the story behind it.

"I don't know if I can call it homeland anymore, honey."

In the latter years of World War II, young German-born Rudy gained US citizenship independent of his immigrant parents and volunteered for air duty. His missions as a B-24 gunner helped conquer the land of his birth, the land of his cherished stepmother, *Mutti*, the land that had captured his papa's loyalty.

"So you don't want to go to Germany?" I ask.

"You know I have to go there. We've talked about it. I promised Mutti I'd visit her family . . . her sisters and my cousins. They're just about all the family I have left. I promised her I'd visit her grave and bring her white roses. I've put it off too long."

On her deathbed in America, Mutti had asked to be returned home to be buried in her village in southern Germany, alongside her brother, a German Air Force crewman killed in the First World War.

Rudy rarely talks about the bombings of World War II, but when he does he bites his lip and brings a hand to his mouth, chewing a single nail. I notice in these months before our trip that in quiet moments he sometimes bites the lip and raises a hand to his mouth. I notice, too, that as our departure gets closer, nightmares come some nights, and his bedding is tangled by morning.

I feel unsettled too, and my sleep is restless. When I wake in the middle of the night I think about the coming trip. World War II was for me a chapter in my history textbook; for Rudy, it was a chapter in his life. Until now, our vacations together have been frivolous escapes from our jobs and our routines. They have been the trips of optimists. This journey plunges us headfirst into painful history.

Saving dollars is a pleasant distraction. Rudy chooses a charter flight distinguished by more than its attractive price—the company uses a card table as its airport check-in counter, has a contact phone number missing two digits, and when its plane, nine hours late, taxies for takeoff, the pilot announces a change in seating.

". . . Too many people back of plane. Quick, some go front."

I stay awake for the entire twelve-hour flight. Someone needs to stay vigilant in these long cross-ocean flights. Pilots get sleepy. In particular, I pray that passengers are well distributed for landing and that my Depression-era mate turns into a bon vivant when he lands in Europe.

Prayer number one answered; prayer number two not. I wait outside the Frankfurt terminal while Rudy picks up a rental car from a local budget firm. When he finally drives up, our convertible gray Citroen cowers behind sub-compact Fords. When I stand next to it, the well-used vehicle barely rises above my waist. Its backseat doubles as a trunk and its doors seem to be made of plastic. Yet another prayer: may truck drivers on the autobahns be observant.

We begin this day a ritual that will endure in our annual European travel: Rudy will drive; I will navigate. There are reasons for this. I do not understand stick shift and he does not believe in maps.

"Maps are good for general concepts," he says. "Better to rely on intuition, inspiration." Translated, this means an itinerary from Rome to Florence under Rudy's navigation someday might include Paris.

"Where are we staying tonight?" I ask, instantly realizing that is a question better posed a month ago at home. I needn't worry, though, about autobahns. We turn onto the first country road we see. Farmhouses and cottages, but no hotels in sight.

"Look for a *zimmer frei* sign, usually on a mailbox," Rudy says. "Means free room, not free price, unfortunately. Free as in available."

AFTER a night in the extra bedroom of Mathilde, we drive several hours south to visit Mutti's and Rudy's families. He has never met these relatives in person and has only a postcard sent last month in response to his letter. It says, *Willkommen.*

At home, six thousand miles away from Germany, our reunion did not seem so difficult to me as it does today. At home, I thought the challenge would be Rudy's, not mine. At home I thought thirty-five years' distance from the war could be enough for towns to heal. Being here only a day, I know how wrong I was. We are astounded at the amount of recon-struction that has already taken place, but still, rebuilding continues—new housing, roadways, bridges, and homes for disabled veterans. In a few places we see "before" and "after" photos mounted on newly erected churches or town halls: "Before" is the building leveled to the ground; "After" is the restoration. We observe that buildings are more easily re-stored than people, as we sometimes see men of Rudy's age sitting on park benches or at bus stops. They have lost arms, or legs, or spirit.

As the images come one after another, Rudy repeats what he says often at home: "There was no choice, Mare. It was a war that had to be."

I have asked this question at home, but now I need to ask it again. "Are you sure these relatives really understand that you were in these bombing raids over their country?"

"It's not likely a secret that a family can keep, honey. The older women probably learned eventually." Then, with a break in his voice, he tries to assure me. "Don't worry. Mutti was lovable and good. I've told you she was perfect . . . and she loved me. That's what will be important to them. And re-member, for almost three years after the war, our every spare dollar went to buy emergency food and supplies to ship to them. I would help Mutti and Papa pack up big cartons every single week and carry them to the postal service. These peo-ple will remember, Mare."

This is typical Rudy, confident in his beliefs, expecting that things will work out well. I just hope he is right this time.

We pull into a parking place directly in front of the address, go to the heavy door, and knock one of those tentative knocks that says, "We hope this is okay." There is no response. Rudy knocks a bit more assertively, and I ready myself to run if needed. At last an elderly woman answers the door. She looks surprised, alarmed even, and turns to call loudly and harshly to someone behind her, leaving us at the open door.

"*Schnell, das Telefon, telefonieren Angelica. Schnell.*"

I look to Rudy who remembers a few German words, "*schnell*" among them. "It means quickly, do something very quickly," he explains.

Apparently a woman named Angelica is being summoned by phone and must come quickly. I have the plot worked out in my head: someone inside has had a heart attack, they are expecting Angelica the nurse, and instead here we are on their doorstep, foreign intruders, enemies in war. Bad timing. I move closer to Rudy, glance up and see he has a broad smile. "This older woman must be my aunt."

Meanwhile, I am, without thinking, slowly moving back from the door, inching closer to our car, when a young lady dressed in a simple dark suit comes hurrying down the street. The older woman steps outside to wave her in. "*Angelica, Angelica.*"

Slowly, we realize we are the emergency and Cousin Angelica the cure. In her arms is a giant book, an inches-thick dictionary titled *English to German and German to English.* Smiles all around, the welcome begins anew. Inside, Angelica takes off her coat and hat, sits at the head of a large wooden table, and dons thick spectacles. She is ready for words.

One by one we meet the family, two of Rudy's aunts and

uncles and three of his cousins, each of them greeting us with hugs or handshakes and Angelica translating as needed. I understand *willkommen,* welcome, and know *danke schön* means thank you, but beyond that I am isolated by language. Rudy has told me often that his German vocabulary is limited to a four-year-old's experience; however, that is not what I conclude tonight. In the kitchen of his German family, his words flow. He knows when to laugh at their jokes, when to raise a stein in another toast, when to pat a back. I move to the edges of the group, smiling when anyone glances at me. As kind as they are, I cannot belong here in the same way he does. My relief that he has been so embraced overtakes my envy of the linguists.

The older woman who had come to the door, one of the aunts, brings in platter after platter of beef stroganoff and *spaetzle* noodles, vegetables, and sweets. Her son wheels in a cart with beers and wines from the region. They seat me right in the middle of the group—someone must have seen me on the edges. They make sure my wine glass is never empty. With Angelica's help, the son invites us to the brewery and vineyard tomorrow. "You are *willkommen,*" he says.

The next morning, Rudy and I go with the family to visit the graves of his Mutti and her brother lost in combat. We all stand close together for what seems a long time, our heads down. Leaving at last, we place garlands of white roses on the stones.

Once we have toured the town and it is time for us to leave, Angelica looks directly at me and translates the smiles and pats on the back. "They say you both should come back. They say you belong here. You are *willkommen.*"

HEADING north, Hamburg next.

Maybe it is that Mutti's family spoiled us with warmth. Maybe it is that the climate in north Germany is colder than the south. Maybe it is that the north is more industrialized, more down-to-business than the slower-moving south. Or maybe it is that Rudy just has too many ghosts in Hamburg. Whatever the source, the air is chilly here.

At home in California, we laughed about ordering a plaque for Rudy's birthplace, perhaps one like Mozart's in Salzburg or Shakespeare's in Stratford. In the fantasy, Rudy mounts his golden plaque to the door of his papa's saloon, commemorating the night he was delivered in its upstairs apartment by a doctor, a regular customer at the bar. "*Er wurde hier gebornen* Rudolf Simon Jensen 17 Mai 1921."

Now here in Hamburg, the reality of World War II, Rudy's war, prevents that historical birth from being immortalized. Our search for the saloon takes us to the edge of the Reeperbahn, Hamburg's red-light district. It is dusk and ladies of the night are taking their positions in windows of brothels and bars as customers begin to crowd the street. Two policemen patrolling the pedestrian walkway look at us quizzically, then approach. Rudy's disguise—an outfit he assembled in a local thrift store—apparently has not fooled them. I thought the weathered blue captain's cap might mislead them. There is, I suppose, the possibility that, dressed in a California sundress and sandals, I have given us away.

"Hazard," they warn. "Danger." We look around us and

have to agree that the area looks threatening. They have another concern: "Americans?" I suspect they are trying to tell us the threat is greater for Americans, that resentments here could run deep.

"Don't worry," Rudy tries to assure me, "they're talking about pickpockets. Just be careful."

In his mix of German and English, Rudy tries to explain to the officers that he was born here in this neighborhood, that he is looking for his papa's waterfront saloon and its upstairs apartment. He doesn't tell them, but I know he wants to see the upstairs apartment because his mother died there two years after his birth.

"*Gebornen hier? Gebornen hier? Oh.*" The patrolmen shrug their shoulders, gesture widely. Their body language says, "How could you find such an old place here?" They point to a plaque on one disco bar: "Built 1901, Destroyed 1944, Rebuilt 1949." They point to the sky. The policemen are trying to tell us that the war likely leveled Rudy's birthplace.

"I wonder," Rudy says as the men leave, "do you think those two have any idea that I was in the war, in the war against them?"

"Well, you're American and the age of most veterans, so maybe for awhile they imagined that. But when you told them you were born here, I think they couldn't imagine you had been in the war against them. Their manner changed. They probably saw you as a fellow citizen."

We walk slowly. "You know, I was never asked to fly over Hamburg. I always wondered if that was because my commanders knew it was my birthplace . . . God knows I had written "Hamburg, Germany" as place of birth on a hundred forms . . . or if it was that when I entered the war, there was already too little of Hamburg left to bomb."

There is too much to absorb. What bombs were unable to destroy here, horrific firestorms that followed them did. The city is a mix of careful reconstruction and stark new buildings. We walk along the waterfront until we find a few older structures that have a slim chance of holding Rudy's heritage, but we cannot settle definitively on one.

At the large port we sit on a bench, watching boats dock and unload. Each time a larger ship comes into view, Rudy stands and walks toward it, squinting into the sun and waving. Old habits.

"I was probably about three when I spent so much time at the dock. My mother had been gone about a year . . . and Papa too. All I can understand now as an adult is that when she died, he must have been very depressed. He must have been heartbroken."

I know Rudy's papa sold the saloon, went back to sea, and left him with a foster mom. I have seen the pictures of Rudy the toddler. Posed in a professional studio, the boy with long locks drapes his arm around a dog, or holds hands with a teddy bear. The photos are of a sad boy, one not comforted by either animal.

"My foster mother would bring me here to meet Papa's ship. We'd wait for the longest time to see him come down the gangplank. He was a really big man with heavy whiskers and a canvas bag thrown over one shoulder. He was so big, he scared me every time."

"It must have seemed like a long wait in between his visits—time goes so slowly when you're a kid," I say. "Maybe he scared you because he seemed like a stranger to you each time."

"Could be. But when he picked me up and hugged me, he felt warm. He would stay with us a day or so, and then we would come back to the port to wave good-bye to him."

Rudy turns from me, looks out to sea. "Every time he left, I would cry and he would promise: 'Someday you and I . . . we both go to America.'"

✈

WE have another place to visit in Hamburg. Rudy wants to see a wooded park in the midst of the city, to make sense of bad dreams he has had about the place all his life, dreams about running and running, looking everywhere for someone.

✈

HIS foster mother had a teenage girl, Helge, who helped with babysitting and feeding the toddler. "I loved Helge. She was so nice to me. That's why I think it was all an accident."

We climb up the stairs of the church steeple to a small landing from which we can see the new high-rise buildings of the city and a sprawling, densely wooded park below.

"I think this is the park. We came here nearly every day. I was three or four years old. Helge was teaching me 'hide and seek.' One afternoon I ran ahead of her, leaving her behind. It got darker and darker. But then I was in the middle of thick trees. I ran and ran, in circles probably. When I couldn't find her anywhere, I just lay down and sobbed, calling her name over and over, for so long. It was terrible."

I feel myself choking and try to cover it with a cough. I

can hear the stories and imagine the feelings, but I know I cannot ever fully understand the life of the lost child and the young airman.

He pauses then, starts to smile. "But after so much crying and calling her name, I looked up and saw her running right toward me. She put out her arms and caught me in a big hug. That part was wonderful."

I catch him in a big hug, and after a time, look up at him and ask, "Did you ever try to meet Helge and her mother again, when you were older?"

"Papa and I tried to contact them after the war, to see if they needed our care packages. We wanted to say thank you, but they had disappeared. They were Jewish."

Looking out over the city, I understand that we will often come to this country, but that ours will never be a tourist holiday.

CHAPTER SIX

ITALY
1981
ITALY

YES. IT IS TRUE. I MARRIED HIM. NOW, EXACTLY ONE YEAR after a honeymoon night on the Edinburgh roof, our union is being tested again, this time on the Italian autostrade leading from Rome. Italian drivers, when they choose a rental car, do not test car brakes—they test car horns. The speed of the autostrade explains all that. I will admit that I have, in the last hour, done a bit of screaming. Covering my eyes has not helped, as I can feel the traffic flying around our little car. I cannot help myself; I share driving tips with Rudy.

Rudy, meanwhile, has his own thoughts. "I've been thinking about this a lot today."

I brace myself.

"I worry that we're wasting good time, Mare. We have the same old arguments day after day. They have already gotten boring and repetitive, and we've only been married a year. We don't want to end up like some old couple bickering all day, wasting time."

He has a plan: "Let's take our most frequent complaints and number them, like your comments about my driving. From now on, you can just call out the number. It'll save time."

"Hmmm . . . number one would have to be, 'You're speeding like a madman.' Number two could be, 'You're going the wrong way down a one-way street.'"

I interrupt myself to scream, "One!" This is not a practice session. The numbers save time, it's true, but I already miss full-blooded arguments. We are, after all, in Italy. I lean back in my seat, settling in for a long discussion of the proposed strategy, just as Rudy takes an exit for a hill town not seen on our tourist maps. I don't have time to number my complaint. I think it would have been a "two" except that we are heading down what is not a road at all. There is not even one way, but rather a narrow path from an earlier era, probably meant now for tractors or pedestrians or cattle, clearly not for Ford Fiestas. There is an unfortunate curve behind our car, so backing up is not an option.

The town's laundry hangs above us, strung on clothes-lines extending from home to home. The town's women also hang above us, leaning out their windows, most shaking their fists and yelling something that must translate to 'stupid Americans again,' but others wave and laughingly call out to us. I am mortified.

"What are you going to do now?" I ask Rudy. Even I can hear my panic.

"Find my camera. I have to get a picture of this. What a beautiful passageway. You know it could be from medieval times."

"I mean what will you do now to get us out of here?"

"Oh, don't worry. They'll have a way to help us. We can't be the first dumb tourists here."

He squeezes halfway out the car door, then adjusts his large camera lens and immortalizes the path, the wet laundry, the waving housewives. Everyone now wants to be in the American's film.

His rule about relying on kind strangers holds true again: a farmer atop a tractor appears ahead of us. The man has clearly done this before. He adjusts our mirrors, employs two villagers to guard the sides of the car, and then at about two miles an hour leads us down the curving passageway. Freed at last, Rudy surprises me.

"That was very upsetting," my usually unflappable spouse says.

"No kidding—I thought we were going to spend the rest of our lives in that alley."

"No, I mean it was very upsetting to have the sun in the wrong position for good pictures. They'll look all washed out."

I am not known as the violent type, but that night I write something in my journal about murder.

We recover to explore the hill towns, a beautifully quiet collection of artistic, historic villages. In three days our only unsettling experience is in Assisi, home of Saint Francis, patron of animals. In full view of the famous statue with birds perched upon saintly shoulders, a restaurant chalkboard announces the day's special, pigeon pie.

It is a good thing we rested in the small towns, because our entry into Florence is exhausting. We are barely surviving humid Italian days and Rudy has compromised his rules about traveling on the cheap. He has booked a modern hotel with air conditioning. But where is it? We circle and circle the city, dodging mad Italian drivers and jaywalkers, unable to find any road that might lead to our hotel, reputed to be northeast of town. We stop policemen and they shake their heads; only tourists go in that area. One, two, three hours go by and still we are lost. We begin to recognize the same buildings over and over in our loops around the city. One of the now familiar landmarks is a small bar along a side street near the old bridge. Rudy pulls into the last space in its parking lot, takes a city map, and goes inside, leaving me to do what I do best in crisis—nap.

He returns with a beautiful young woman with vibrant dark eyes and long curling black hair. Before I can ask who she is, he clears a place for her to sit in our backseat.

"Maria, this is Mary. Mary, Maria," he says. "Her boyfriend Marcus is the bartender in there and he loaned her to us."

"He loaned her to us?"

"Right. He loaned her to us. It works out perfectly. Maria

lives out by our hotel and wants to go home. Her boyfriend has to work late tonight. Maria can show us the way. She speaks a little bit of English and, combined with the Italian I learned this week, we'll be fine."

It could have worked out perfectly except that Maria always takes the bus. She has no idea what roads lead home, let alone where our hotel is. To compensate for the knowledge gap, she points out tourist attractions, most of which we have seen five times today. She is helpful, though, in keeping Rudy's driving speed down—she screams and prays loudly as he approaches every intersection. Her English is spotty at best, but we understand her advice, "Bus."

At last there is a miracle. It is good we did not eat the pigeon pie, because the saint is on our side. As we enter a more recent housing development, Maria points to the left and Rudy instinctively turns right. Now, directly in front of us, is our hotel. We look at each other. We can't take Maria home because with or without her we will never find our way back here.

"Come, Maria," Rudy says as he opens her door. "*Grazie, grazie.* We get you good taxi."

It does not take long for us to view Maria's advice as life changing. We park our rental car for the week and find the bus.

A few days later, Maria runs to catch us as we leave the hotel, her long dark curls flying in the morning breeze. She brings tickets to the final match of the *Calcio,* a lively annual competition between neighborhoods of the city. From her combination of hand gestures and English fragments, we understand that Marcus's cousin plays in the historic football game, and that we may sit with their neighborhood if we wear green and cheer only for his team. No, we cannot pay for the tickets; they are to thank us for seeing her home. Rudy and I look at each other guiltily.

Rudy has read about the importance of the game to the city.

"This is serious business, Mare. In the sixteenth century, Florence was once under siege and had to finish the *Calcio* before fighting back."

Entering the arena, we understand just how serious this is. The audience, divided into neighborhood groups by colors, packs bleacher seats and practices deafening cheers.

"*Bella, bella, bella.*"

On the sand field, a procession begins. The two teams of athletes, brandishing muscles and making menacing sounds, are escorted by city fathers clad in brilliantly colored sixteenth-century guild robes. Behind them comes a well-nourished heifer. Again the cheers, this time for the cow.

"*Bella, bella, bella.*"

It is easy to see why the *Calcio* is said to be a combination of every sport except baseball. This historic football game has touches of soccer, kickball, wrestling, and street fighting. In the interest of getting the ball to goal, many maneuvers are approved, including head-butting, punching, and choking. Gurneys line the outfield, ready for business after each brawl. At the end, our winning team—or at least the survivors of our winning team—converge on the field to claim the cow for their/our neighborhood.

On our last day in Florence, after multiple visits to *David* and our favorite gelato café, Rudy and I take a longer bus ride, up the hills above Florence to the small town of Fiesole. Rudy gathers intelligence from the driver about lunch stops. Criteria: cheap prices, hearty food. Our bill for the air-conditioned hotel is mounting, and we have been dining on sandwiches in our room all week.

The bus driver's choice is a large truck stop dating from another century. It is not like the truck stops we know at home, where few if any truck drivers would ever eat. Here the parking lot is filled with pickups to 14-wheelers, the picnic benches inside crowded with customers. White bean soup, spaghetti with meat sauce, and green salad sit in big bowls on each table. Red wine in carafes completes the meal. The fixed price is one fifth of what we pay in town.

"I can tell it's delicious," Rudy says.

Walking back to the bus stop after our meal, we see a frail older man, cane in hand, seated on the bench. Rudy is tired after the large lunch and sits beside him. I begin to walk further up the hill, wondering how one burns off a thousand calories. When I circle back to the bench a few minutes later, Rudy asks if we can wait out the next bus, stay here awhile longer. He and the gentleman, he says, have some things to talk about. A half hour or so later, our bus comes and the two men shake hands, embrace, wave good-bye. On the ride home, Rudy tells me the man is German, his bad leg a war injury.

"It's something I always wondered about, whether this could happen," Rudy says. "We think he was in at least one of the missions I flew. We were probably shooting at each other, Mare, trying to bring the other's plane down. Now we sit to-gether and talk at an Italian bus stop."

"What did you share?"

"What you would guess . . . we shared that we were too young for war, that we just wanted to finish our flights, finish our duty, and go home. We talked a lot about how it was up there. He made promises to himself, too, when it was over. And, I don't know if I should have, but I told him I was born in Hamburg."

"I would think he'd have a hard time understanding how someone born in Hamburg could attack Germany."

Rudy has his head down. "Of course he did."

IT is not easy to leave Italy, either emotionally or physically. We depart from Bari, a seaside port, taking an overnight ferry to Dubrovnik. The next morning, Rudy with his early-rising rule saves us. He wakes me.

"Mare, quick. We've landed in Dubrovnik. But we haven't just landed. We're getting ready to pull out to sea again."

"Hey, what about that wakeup call we signed up for?"

"Forget it . . . throw your coat over your pajamas and run up to the deck. Run. I'll take our cases and try to get our car out of the hold."

"Just don't let them keep me on this boat."

The crew's expressions when I reach the deck say there is no chance they will keep me, the crazed uncombed American woman in pajamas shouting "prob-lem, prob-lem" and clinging to her coat, purse, and shoes. They move the boat back to the pier.

Chapter Seven

YUGOSLAVIA
1981
YUGOSLAVIA

I HAVE SAT ON RUDY'S SUITCASE THREE TIMES NOW AND STILL cannot conquer the bulges.

My voice is shrill, which is how it gets when, the night before an international flight, the luggage will not close.

"There is no way this book can come with us, Rude. It's

three inches thick and the size of a tabletop. And do you know how much it weighs?"

Rudy considers. "It probably weighs a lot. Tito had a full life. You know he was eighty-seven when he died last year."

He launches into a summary of the man's life from Resistance leader to president, but I need to get to the point. "Rudy, tourists do not bring Yugoslavian history books with them into the country. They buy them there to read. Probably because they weigh so much."

"But that's a chance we can't take. What if I don't find this in English? And where am I going to get a price lower than the used bookstore here? I bet there's a run on this book over there."

THE customs agent begins to riffle through our papers and luggage, looking at us with suspicion. "You here business? pleasure?"

"Neither," I want to say, but Rudy is ready with his answer.

"Pleasure, sir, pleasure to see your country."

When the official comes across the Tito biography, he pulls it from the bottom of the case, holds it high, and smiles at me. Then he pats Rudy on the back and helps us repack our case, sending us through the Green Light lane.

We find Yugoslavia a mix of beautiful sights and consumer frustrations, a blend not unusual in socialist countries. Dubrovnik is perhaps the most dramatically sited city I have ever seen. Our room is small and simple, but it has the view we came for: red-tiled structures and walls jutting out to sea.

We walk the ramparts each day, see the tiles from above, watch as fishermen pull small wooden boats laden with catch onto the shore. Each afternoon when we come back from our walk, we are pleased to see the hotel still standing. Building maintenance does not seem high on the government priority list: paint peels, elevators stop between floors, door frames lean.

There is a do-it-yourself quality to this hotel, as guests appear to be on their own. The first night the dining room is dark, empty at six o'clock. Rudy finds the desk clerk and asks, "Restaurant no open? Dark, all dark." While I blush, he illustrates by flicking the switch for the desk area up and down. "Dark, see dark."

"Yes, restaurant open." The clerk points to his watch. "Seven? Eight? Nine?" He is asking us a question, not making a statement. Tonight and every night of our week here, we skip the darkened hotel restaurant and find a fisherman's family seated around a portable barbecue and an eight-by-eleven-inch hand-lettered sign that reads "Café Fish." We eat grilled fish we will long dream of.

We don't have time to sit and look at Dubrovnik's red-tiled roofs for days, or we would. On the road to Split, we drive in circles, lost and tired, finally stopping at an advertised government resort for the night. The luxurious façade is just that. Inside we locate and fill out our own tourist cards, persuade a bellman to find us an empty room, and pour our own drinks at the bar. We bribe a young woman, perhaps a guest, to be our waitress.

We eventually make our way to a ferry that takes us over the bluest of Adriatic waters, then drive on to the town of

Bled, high in the Julian Alps. Any traveler we meet along the way insists we spend time at Lake Bled. It is, they say, extraordinarily beautiful and romantic. We are not disappointed by the emerald lake and its church that sits with its steeple atop a rocky island. We are in fact so taken with the sight that we throw Rudy's budget rule to the wind and check into a beautiful old hotel, netting a room facing it all.

"What say we never leave here?" Rudy calls from the terrace. "I'm less than a third of the way through the Tito book." Leaving it on the outdoor table, we go down to breakfast. After our meal and a walk along the easy lakeside path, we return to our room to find a handmade lace cloth covering our table. I finger the lace, the careful stitches. On our budget we are not used to the fineries of travel.

On day two, we walk again, longer this time, and on the path meet a dozen men and women, brown-skinned from laboring under a bright sun, headed now we guess for a wedding in the church. On this hot, humid day, each woman wears a black or navy pleated wool skirt, a heavy sweater, and a kerchief. Men wear the wool in pants and jackets. They all have sturdy black shoes, carry small gift packages, and show us broad smiles and missing front teeth. Their gestures toward the lake say, "Isn't it all beautiful?"

We return for lunch at the hotel. While we are gone we have become celebrities. "Are you the people on the second story with that decorated terrace?" fellow tourists ask, scarcely hiding their envy.

They take us to the lawn behind the hotel where we can view all the terraces. All except ours have an unadorned plastic table and two plastic chairs. Indeed, our lacy tablecloth has been joined by a large ceramic bowl of fruit and a garland of brightly colored fresh flowers. Walking into our room, we find the Tito book in the center of our coffee table, opened to a full-page photo of him as president. He has merited a garland of flowers too.

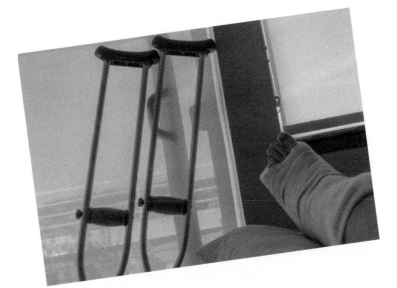

Chapter Eight

SPAIN AND 1982 PORTUGAL

WE HAVE BEEN ON THE ROAD FOR MORE THAN A MONTH in Spain. So much tourist literature highlights central Europe that we are unprepared for the elegance and beauty of this country. To see its vast terrain, we have to do what we are not so good at—tour all day and stay one, at most two, nights in simple inns, packing and unpacking, sensing that in our hurry to move on we are leaving more than the stray toothbrush behind. Life, though, has a way of slowing you down.

Our subcompact rental car chugs up mountain passes and skirts through cities with never a problem. Until there is a big one. We are in a long, long tunnel, driving in the far right lane with traffic racing around us in three lanes to our left, speeding toward what must be light at the end, when our Ford shudders and stops. Just stops. Rudy tries again and again to coax it to life, but not a whimper comes from under the hood.

Spaniards have good reflexes: they dart around us, rolling down windows to shout what is either helpful advice or a Spanish version of road rage. After approximately three years and two months, a car pulls in front of us and its brave passenger jumps out briefly, long enough to gesture to our hood and point to a bright red telephone on the opposite tunnel wall. We raise the hood and dodge three lanes of cars and trucks to reach the red phone and a relatively safe, narrow, concrete platform. I am prepared—I clutch my purse with our passports and our California automobile club card.

The voice on the other end of the line speaks loudly, excitedly. "Allo, allo."

I do the same. "Allo, allo. Tunnel. In tunnel. Car no go, Triple A," I say.

"Allo, allo. Tunnel? No go?" she repeats, her puzzled tone suggesting this is not understandable input.

"Help me, *Aidez-moi*," I say over and over, drawing upon all the languages I know, Spanish unfortunately not among them.

The operator and I continue to get acquainted while Rudy runs along the concrete edge, gesturing wildly, trying to slow cars. Suddenly we see across the lanes a police car pulling up behind our Ford, lights flashing and bringing traffic to a halt. Red lights flash outside the tunnel now too, apparently signaling oncoming cars not to enter. This must be some sort of automatic system triggered by lifting the phone; gratefully, my linguistic skills do not determine our fate. A tow truck appears, and the police gesture us to cross in front of the stopped rows of traffic and climb into its cab. Our crippled car grasps a tow bar and off we go.

The light is at the end of the tunnel, but it is slightly dimmed. From what we can understand from the mechanic who arrives, the Ford's needed part is not available within one hundred kilometers. Our tow driver refuses to abandon us, so we three sit on a curb outside the repair shop, waiting hours in the heat while the part makes its way by air-conditioned taxi. It is a convenient system: the cab arrives, the tow driver lifts the precious part from its backseat into the repair shop, then tow driver, taxi driver, Rudy, and I head to the nearest bar.

There is little to talk about while time and car repair go by. We share no language other than gestures and an interest in Rudy's knockoff Rolex watch ($21 from a lower Manhattan street merchant).

"I have to get this across, that it is imitation, Mare," Rudy whispers. "I can't let them think I can afford a real one."

"I'm buying you a kid's Timex in the morning."

We needn't have worried. The costliest part of our expenses is our bar bill.

IT is time for a slowed down, restful beach vacation. No traffic or tunnels for us for awhile. We head south to Portugal's slower pace and dramatic Algarve beaches. Passing by more recently developed resort towns, we select a small seaside village where a few inns sit side by side with colorful open-air cafés, and just behind rows of small, brightly painted fishing boats pulled up onto the sand. From our deck, Rudy can watch the boats come in and the tuna fishermen untangle their nets over the afternoon's first beer. Actually, he can't just watch. Packing up his tattered towel, old hat, and worn sandals, Rudy moves down to the beach. When I join him an hour or so later, he is enjoying his second beer.

"Hon, I found the most charming, *authéntico* little bar. Really nice people."

He points up the hill to a bungalow where a dozen or more fishermen stand on a concrete porch enjoying their beverages. "I can get you a drink and put it on my tab. I didn't have a wallet but they said that was okay."

I have coins and small bills in my money belt and walk with him to pay his tab and start one of my own. Several men standing inside seem to know Rudy—they pat him on the back and gesture for him to open the large, old refrigerator, saying something like "Help American." I look around for a cash register, a waitress, an owner—anything that would say this is a bar. Nothing does. Everything says it is a home: two children watching TV in a living area, a woman making soup on the stove, the fishermen enjoying a friend's hospitality.

Rudy and I insist on paying for our drinks, but our insistence is ignored as they press two more bottles in our hands. "Help American," they say.

The week goes by. Rudy has figured out a way to keep going to his favorite bar, bringing a six-pack each time to restock the refrigerator.

One of his Rules is in full force here. Blinds are drawn back at bedtime so the sun wakes him early for a daily beach walk. As he leaves each morning, he closes the curtains and I continue to sleep. I am impressed with his new fitness routine, but I don't want to be like him. I wake slowly this morning and, just as I step out onto our balcony, I hear a familiar screech.

"Ahhhh . . . Oouw . . . Dammit . . ."

The last time I heard that cry was when Rudy's favorite college team, the Oregon Ducks, lost a football championship in the final three minutes of their game. This is how agony sounds.

I dress rapidly and follow the scream that is fading gradually to a pitiful yelp. Five men stand in a circle over a body sitting on the sand. One of the men knows me, as we met yesterday. I trust he has explained to the others that I am the wife of the guy who mistook his beachfront bungalow for a public bar. The man looks at me sympathetically now.

Rudy, seated in the center of the circle, holds a big toe that seems to be turning purple. He sees me and points indignantly at the culprit, a large, jagged rock formation sticking far out of the sand. The men exchange looks among themselves. Then they point as one to a volleyball game taking place beside the rock, and wait with their heads down while I comprehend the situation. The volleyball players are tall, bronzed, shapely women. Tall, bronzed, *topless* shapely women. Have you ever wanted to feign sympathy but found it impossible?

We frequently meet new teachers who ask to sit with us at meals. They are expected to teach English in the schools but know little of the practical language. Tourists are their training ground, idioms and slang phrases their delight.

Pointing to Rudy's bandaged foot, one young teacher asks sympathetically, "What is it you call that in America? Accident, accidental?"

I clarify. "In America, we call it Fitting Punishment. We call it Justice."

Even with Rudy on crutches for a broken toe and sprained foot, Portugal and the Portuguese enchant us. Each night after a grilled fish dinner on the beach, we take a taxi to a nightclub with *fado* singers to hear haunting, mournful songs about poverty, death, the unforgiving, murderous sea, and the glory that was once *Lisboa*. After a few nights, we know enough refrains to be able to hum in the chorus of patrons. Rudy with his handicap finds some comfort in communal sadness. I cry with the audience sometimes. There is something universal, something cleansing in the sad songs.

Chapter Nine

CZECHO-SLOVAKIA
1983

THIS IS MY FAULT. FOR ONCE I AM NOT ABLE TO BLAME Rudy for plunging us into drama and risk. Instead, it was I who drew the line on the map from the rent-a-car office in Frankfurt, Germany, straight to Prague, Czechoslovakia. I am looking for my roots.

The grandfather I had never met was born and raised in the region. I visualize the country populated by my cousins, equally unknown, and I suspect that if my inner bohemian is ever to emerge it will be as I stand in the middle of Charles Bridge. Grandfather left the bridge one day eighty years earlier and immigrated to America. My own father could tell me little about the man. The last time he had seen him was when, at age ten, he said good-bye to the near-stranger in the bowler hat and shiny black suit who boarded a train headed for Deadwood, South Dakota, and to all accounts, a career in gambling and selling worthless gold-mining stocks. I have higher expectations of a bohemian life (think strumming guitar and writing poetry) and cannot stop humming on my way to the land of my kinsmen.

My father had told me of Czechoslovakia's noble history—national monuments rivaling those in London and Paris, contributions to the worlds of education, opera, and literature. But as Rudy and I approach the border, my humming slows to a stop. The stark gates and barren fields do not evoke memories of Dvořák or Renaissance glory. Instead, we face evidence of the Soviet invasion fifteen years earlier: the Soviet hammer and sickle embroidered on the sole flag and upon the jackets of the machine-gun-armed guards. We would learn more in Prague, but for now we judge that the Soviets are successfully squelching Czech resistance and liberalization.

We take our place in line before a twenty-foot-high gate, maneuvering our tiny, red, dusty Ford Fiesta behind a military convoy, eleven new and shiny tanks that each rise a full story above us. After a cursory look at our car, a guard gestures us to drive ahead.

"That was easy," I say prematurely, stopping my sentence

short when I realize we are not being sent through the border crossing; we are being directed onto a side lane where a half dozen armed young Soviet guards begin to inspect our car, our visas, and our state-arranged hotel reservations. Of particular interest is an envelope they find in the bottom of the glove compartment showing the return address "Frankfurt American High School/APO NY." We have visited Elisabeth and Robert, friends who teach for the U.S. Department of Defense. We are suspects, and the small map of Prague I have torn from a tourist book is further clear evidence of our ill intent. The inspectors are perhaps eighteen or nineteen years old and have the eyes of heavy drinkers. Their two-hour ceremony of furrowed brows, dismayed looks, and shaking heads continues until at last The General arrives to confer, and in a gesture that I swear is akin to a papal blessing, waves us through the gates.

But being cleared for entrance does not mean the end of stress. The Fiesta has been showing low levels of petrol since the last town, where the station pumps had run dry. We had looked forward to reaching this border area, confident we would find a supply of petrol in the government-run stations and still reach our hotel in Prague by nightfall.

Victory! Once clear of the border gate, we can see a station with attendants busily filling the tanks of freight trucks. We pull the Fiesta into line and Rudy grabs his wallet with its collection of currencies and traveler's checks to be shared generously with the station man.

The clerk knows just enough German to clarify. "Russian money good. Czech money good."

Rudy knows the same amount of German. "Have Deutsche

Marks, German money, good money. And dollars. Good money U.S. You know U.S.?"

That is the wrong question. They know too much about the U.S.

Rudy also knows the international language of bribery. He waves bills before the clerk, but there is no compromising the man's communist ideals.

He insists, "German no good. Dollar no good."

"Have traveler's checks."

"Checks okay. Go bank to cash."

Rudy looks about and asks, "Where is bank?"

"No. No bank here."

"Where IS bank? Have no petrol."

"Next town. Far."

Rudy in a crisis is not above self-humiliation. He gestures to his eyes, pantomiming the sadness and tears that would arise from being stranded the rest of his life at the Czech border. Then he points to me and I realize he is saying it is my tears that will flow. In truth, it does not take much for my eyes to fill at that very moment, and two or three tears begin to descend my cheeks. This is not acting.

I pull from my pocket a small map I had secreted from the guards and locate the nearest town some fifty kilometers away, unfortunately in the opposite direction from Prague. We get back into the car, see the gas needle lying flat on the dashboard, and take time for the briefest of spats.

Rudy is ready for a prison break. "We drive to that little town as fast as we can, get money, get petrol, and make Prague tonight."

I have been taught this as a teen with a first car. "Driving fast uses up your petrol fast. We go slowly, spend the night there, and head early tomorrow for Prague."

On our fifty-kilometer trek, I do what I do. I count my deep breaths: "In through the nose, 1 . . . 2 . . . 3 . . . Relax . . . out slowly through the mouth . . . 1 . . . 2 . . . 3 . . . Relax."

Somehow, the tiny town not only has a bank, but a petrol station, an inn, and the only Chinese restaurant we are to see all summer. We toast our good fortune with what seems like very strong white wine, forgetting for the moment that we are now officially missing—missing from our state-arranged hotel in Prague, that is.

The next morning the road heading east to Prague looks like any other quiet, rural highway, with lush green crops on either side.

"This looks like an ordinary, normal road . . . not any guard stations in sight," I say. "After yesterday, I didn't know what to expect."

"Well, Prague must just be different than that border area. More sophisticated."

We slow to a stop at an intersection at the outside edge of the city. Coming literally from nowhere, two armed soldiers step directly in front of us, rifles pointed to our car. There is only one thing worse than two armed soldiers pointing rifles at you, and that is two drunken armed soldiers pointing rifles at you. Drunken soldiers do not hold their weapons steady. They are young and know no English and little German, but we understand it is paperwork they want, so from the cavern of my purse I produce our Czech government visas, passports, and prepaid hotel vouchers from the state travel agency. After looking briefly at the documents, and being openly amused at our passport photos, they wave us forward.

IRONICALLY, our stark, aged hotel is located on Wenceslas Square, directly in the middle of what six years later was to become the hub of the Velvet Revolution, the site of countless demonstrations that marked the transition from years of Soviet control to Czech independence. But on this day, the day of our arrival, there is no sign of ferment and no gatherings. As a seasoned shopper, the first thing I notice is that windows in nearby storefronts are nearly empty. The doorman, clad in a shabby navy topcoat and black pants, opens our car doors and extends his hand for our keys. Rudy and I exchange a look that says, "This might be the last time we see this little car. Take everything out." As we move through an empty lobby to the registration area, the clerk behind the desk begins striking the bell on the counter, then picks up the phone and quietly communicates. Time moves on, but his eyes never rise to see us until at last a taller man appears, dressed in a newer suit and with a name badge that seems to say Manager. He speaks some German and is direct. "You late. Give Veesas, passport."

The documents disappear into his inside jacket pocket. Like the rental car, we hope to see them again someday.

"And our room key?" Rudy asks.

A bellhop is summoned and given a room key; we are not.

The manager explains, "Key safe with hotel."

Our room is tiny but equipped with the essential bed and bathroom. Rudy tests out the latter and reports to me.

"Hey, honey, this toilet has a special feature. It overflows with every flush."

The essentials of the room do not include a phone. When we find the manager downstairs he explains that no, we cannot change rooms, that our room is government-selected. This does not make us happy, and probably to get the disgruntled Americans out of his lobby, he directs us two doors down to the state tourist bureau. We enter a large office space, with a row of clerks seated behind windows, somewhat like our Social Security offices back home. But this office has a level of customer service beyond any Social Security office: before we can identify ourselves, a voice booms out of the quiet.

"Mr. and Mrs. Jensen. Welcome."

I whisper to Rudy, "Are we the only Americans in this city?"

The tourist office welcome unfortunately does not include a room with a functioning toilet, since ours is a special guest room. Indeed, it would be a long week, we would make the hotel handyman our best friend, and to Rudy's credit he would last four days before he asks me, "Are you sure you're related to these people?"

Walking into the hotel dining room that first evening, we note that the dining area is in some contrast to our dingy hotel room. It is old European, with pleasantly faded murals on the walls, white tablecloths, unlit candles, and floral-patterned china. We are eating early and so are not alarmed that there is only one other couple in the dining room. We should have been.

The menu is large and heavy, leather bound and written

in Czechoslovakian but with tiny photos that illustrate some offerings. Rudy ventures to do the ordering in his bilingual fashion, first in English, then attempting German for good measure.

"We will each have a small salad and a beefsteak."

"So sorry. No beef."

"Roast chicken."

"So sorry. No chicken."

"Pork?"

"So sorry."

Rudy decides to play the ordering game differently. "Tell us what you have. Tell us what is in the kitchen."

The waiter grows quiet as he apparently searches for a memory of food in the kitchen.

Time for another strategy. We point to the other couple across the room, asking what they are eating. Yes, we could love spaghetti with some sort of red on top, with its accompanying salad best described as slice of tomato over slice of lettuce.

Cleaning our plates, we look up to see the waiter bringing a platter of large fruit *kolaches*, the traditional Czech pastry my grandmother used to make. Maybe I do belong here after all. I vow that this week I will go to a phone booth, look up my very Czech maiden name, and start calling until I find family.

Surely you know to be careful what you wish for. Rudy does not and he continues to wish for beef and that is a mistake. Our second evening in the dining room, the waiter beams as he announces he has one beefsteak for a lucky guest. That night Rudy is as ill as one can be when one wishes for the last beefsteak in a Czechoslovakian food shortage. The hotel doctor brings potions and prescribes three days' bed rest with tea and rice. While Rudy heals, I venture out into Prague.

THE fourth of July. I am walking the streets of Prague, seeing what I am seeing, yet in some overlay of images, picturing my California neighbors in their red, white, and blue t-shirts, opening packages of hot dogs, lighting barbecues, and talking of fireworks and music from the Capitol Mall. I don't know that last year or any other year I spent time on July Fourth thinking of freedom, but this year I can think of little else.

Banners with the Soviet red hammer and sickle advertise a peace conference in Prague later this summer. Perhaps in preparation, prominent shop windows educate residents about American life, with photos of U.S. air bases, missiles, the Viet Nam war, the Kent State deaths, and the Watts riots. The twenty-year-old photographs are neatly labeled in Czech and in English: "News of America." In the background, tall apartment houses rise gray and dingy, with laundry hanging from windows and balconies. A few black-market money changers appear from alleyways. The occasional dark-windowed limousine drives by, reminding me there is aristocracy even in socialism.

On major street corners, teenage Soviet soldiers hold AK-47s at the ready, but the crowds of shoppers seem to ignore them, grasping nylon net shopping bags and walking resolutely toward stores with empty shop windows. After a week in the city, I will conclude that during shortages Prague women shop all day, not because there is so much, but because there is so little. One must be at the small grocers' stores when deliveries of oranges or coffee arrive, or at the druggist when toiletries appear. Lines form outside in anticipation, and what I have heard seems true—you come not to purchase a specific item but to buy whatever there is in the quantity the clerk allows. The successful shopper may have extra lemons or sanitary napkins to trade with a neighbor for sugar or toilet paper. Standing in the bakery line, I recognize the flowery scent all around me, the scent of my grandmother. Clearly there has been a recent abundance of rosewater cologne.

As I leave our hotel room earlier that morning, Rudy's request for plain crackers and tea bags seems reasonable; hours later I understand it is an impossible dream. My own hope of finding deodorant and laundry soap would have to be postponed until I have time to stand in another line in front of another drug store.

The next day, Rudy is nearly ready for Prague, but the doctor and I are able to convince him to rest another day. I have been careful not to share details of armed soldiers and the anti-American displays I have seen. Instead, I am compliant as he reviews Rule Number Three, letting him choose my most plain and gray attire for the day, clothes that might blend into the city backdrop. I take deep breaths, realizing that he and I have for just a few days changed roles and that already I am ready to give up the Adventurer persona.

Genetics are, however, a powerful force. Gathering a few shreds of determination, I set out to find a phone book and my cousins. Our government-provided hotel does not allow me to view its telephone directory, but in subway stations I find phone booths, one of which has a six-inch phone book, the size of any major city directory, minus the yellow pages of capitalism. And, as I had suspected, I must be related to many of the faces I see on the streets. While at home, our family name is typically two or three listings in a phone book, here page after page holds the name or variations. Like it or not, I am home.

I make my first attempts at contact, choosing to call those with the first name of a family hero: Uncle Anton, who had raised our father after Grandfather left.

Whether I say "hello" or "*prochin*" to the Antons, the response is the same—a loud click from the other end, or a definitive No. When I sense they understand English, I try explaining I am family, have the same name. Then the click.

I dare to ask "Do you speak English?" to some and the click comes faster. My spirit wavers more with each call, and I find myself saying "good-bye" or "thank you" even when there has been no exchange.

Head down, I walk back to tell Rudy of my failure.

"As soon as I say the word 'English' they say 'No' and hang up."

"Why do you think that happens?"

"Well, I'm guessing they're angry and don't want to be interrupted. Maybe they don't get many phone calls and they're startled."

"Or . . . ?"

"Or they could be old, sick . . ."

"Or?"

"Or . . . I don't like to think about this . . . they could be afraid. Do you think they're afraid?"

"Afraid to have an American relative? Why not be afraid?"

At twilight, I walk the streets again, looking more intently this time at those I pass. Finally, it is their eyes that dissolve me, and dissolve my planned reunions. The eyes of my cousins are gray, staring, fearful.

✈

MY mate awakens early the next morning, a new man with the old Rudy vigor.

"Up and at 'em, babe. It's time to be tourists in Prague."

We explore Castle Hill, its one-of-a-kind beautiful monuments and art collections. Today with a bit of sunshine and Rudy healed, I am able to visualize the buildings without their soot layers and to realize they are world treasures. We find Charles Bridge, following the strains of guitars strummed by long-haired young men, dissidents perched on the rails between statues. One statue commemorates the first Northern European university founded here, just one reminder of Prague's noble heritage.

With that heritage buried so deeply under Soviet control, it is impossible for us to guess that in six years Czechoslovakia will be transformed again, when the nation's artists orchestrate the peaceful Velvet Revolution and turn back communist control. We do not recognize them that day, but the clues are here: the young armed soldiers keep a distance (perhaps respectful) from the guitarists, and as we turn to leave the bridge, we hear echoes of Western music.

✈

RUDY is humming, packing to leave Czechoslovakia in the morning. I am too nervous to think clearly and end up scattering my belongings across the room, packing and repacking.

"What are you so worried about?" he asks. "Sure, getting into the country was a little, uh, difficult, but we made it. Why would leaving be hard? I'll even find gas before we go."

I do some preventative planning for escape day, spending most of our Czech currency, throwing away anything that looks like maps of the city, and postponing journal writing until we are safely beyond the border. Yet catastrophic scenarios continue to play in my mind.

"Well, they could find Czech coins we lost track of and jail us for currency theft . . . or they could kidnap us for a prisoner exchange."

My vision of departure day is a bit closer to reality than Rudy's. The shortages had escalated so dramatically that stores are almost empty and spending out our currency is a challenge. I buy stale chocolate bars from the hotel clerk for ten times the going rate; Rudy presses a generous if forbidden tip into the palm of our housekeeper; and in the end we spend our last currency to ransom a dusty, button-eyed cloth doll sitting alone in the back corner of a seamstress's window, dressed in a blue babushka and white pinafore. She has been a legal resident of California for over thirty years now.

Departure morning drags on: checking out of the hotel and retrieving our car and passports consumes an hour, the gasoline line another hour, and then, on the rural roads to the border, we are stopped twice by police cars. In the first stop, I am settling into the passenger seat and beginning to untangle the worn seat belt when a car behind us swerves and moves within inches of me. The uniformed man has noted the "D" for West Deutschland on the license of our rental car and, in a combination of German and gestures, he clarifies the problem.

"No seat belt. See passports."

When he realizes we are Americans, he gleams and reaches deep in his jacket pocket to pull out a handful of papers. From the stack, he selects one for me: a handwritten, well-used note that says "Fine. US Dollar 8." He holds out his hand.

I have noted in the past that on occasion my fear turns to anger and I mutter some words my mother would be ashamed of. This is one of those occasions. Rudy takes charge, ending the conflict by opening his wallet and handing bills to the man. "Need receipt, receipt," he insists, and the original ticket comes back to us, now with some large letters on it. Presumably, we have an autograph.

Within minutes, a second police car stops us and we become another eight dollars poorer. This time we have entered a one-way alley in the wrong direction, gone one hundred yards, then turned around. But entering is the crime. Rudy in a burst of basic German tells the officer/bandit that this is the last ticket police will give us, or that we will have to tell our country. Right. We don't know why the harassment stops. Perhaps Rudy's anger impresses them or there is an industry standard for how many times in one morning a foreigner should be ticketed, or, simply, they don't want us to tell our country.

An American couple we met in Prague had recommended we leave from this smaller, rural border exit, as they had had an easy entry to the country here compared to our frightening experience at the major crossing. This border, however, harbors some secrets. As we approach the small, old guardhouse we count twenty-three large, new 18-wheeler trucks, each filled with ripe and beautiful produce. While Prague women stand in line at their shops, hoping for a few fresh oranges, the best of their country's peaches, berries, and vegetables are leaving through a small border exit in search of foreign currency.

Three young Soviet soldiers collect our passports for review and begin what looks like a routine riffling through our trunk. Routine until one of them inspects the compartment under the luggage near the spare tire. He pulls out a plastic bag, holds a handful of Tampax aloft, and yells for his comrades. We learn that there is a resemblance between Tampax and dynamite and that we and the tubes need more thorough review. When Rudy looks to me to help him explain, I am sitting on a worn bench, my legs collapsed under me, and my head down in an attempt to find some oxygen. Rudy is left alone to repeatedly explain the items are for "the *frau*" in "the month." When the guards begin to understand and blush, and as Rudy offers to give a demonstration, the trunk is closed rapidly.

Just one more hurdle. My passport photo, taken years earlier and before harrowing travel with Rudy, shows a young, healthy woman with makeup and a wide smile. I have to admit there is little resemblance to the Me I present at the guardhouse. Worse, I am Czech and I look Czech; that is, I look this day as if I may be a countrywoman seeking escape with a crazed American tourist. I need to stay on my resting bench while Rudy sorts this out. I put my head down again and hear a flurry of German, first in arguing tones, and then some lightness. My hero, bowing slightly, retrieves me from the bench and hands me my stamped passport. We set off slowly driving through the guard gate.

"How ever did you manage that?" I ask. "I thought I was going to live in Czechoslovakia all my days."

"It was simple. I just told them that if they had had the hard travel you had, they would look this old and ugly too."

Chapter Ten

BERLIN
1983
EAST GERMANY

I AM NERVOUS. EVEN OUR ROAD MAP FLAUNTS THE FRACTURE: a thick red line cutting in half one country, one capital. The Germanys are East and West, split in half, spoils of war. The two halves meet at a tall wall dividing countrymen and families. Studying routes from Czechoslovakia to West Berlin, I remember warnings from tourists: "Be careful. The corridor roads in and out of the city are supposed to be open to all travelers, but remember, Soviets occupy East Germany." East Germany surrounds the eastern corridors.

"It can't be that bad, Mare. We'll stay alert. We'll find the corridor easily. It's bound to be well marked."

Apparently we did not stay alert, not to our fuel level, nor to road signs labeling the transit corridor we should have taken. The "BDR" exit is meant for us, but, convinced we are already on the safe route, we drive on, happily spotting a one-pump gas station along the road. None too soon. We pull up to the pump. The worker, a thin, elderly man, gesticulates wildly and points to our rental car license plate with its bold "D" from West Germany, then begins to scream.

"What's he saying? What's he yelling?" I beg Rudy to translate but Rudy has turned ashen.

At last he can speak. "He's saying something like, 'My God, man, what are you doing here? Get out. Get out. You will be arrested.' I'm not sure I got that translation exactly right."

Close enough. But we can't leave; we've got to get fuel. Rudy takes a moment to pat my arm, look into my watery eyes. "Don't worry. Just a little mistake—we must be in East Germany, the occupied part. It will all work out."

This is the way it works out: the kind attendant hears our despair, rushes to give us a few liters of petrol, then gestures that we must go and go now. He does not want our coins, as he cannot use West German money. He only wants us to leave. Rudy stuffs a few dollar bills in the man's shirt pocket, races to the driver's seat, and we are off. It is a half hour (more like fifty-five hours) before we spot the sign announcing an upcoming corridor roadway. On the way to that blessed junction, we watch our rearview mirror for any police cars following us, debating which is the better approach to a successful escape. I want to speed to the exit, shortening the time of terror. Rudy thinks a slow, measured pace attracts less attention.

Neither of us is prepared for what happens around a twisting bend in the road: a Soviet soldier, holding a rifle, steps out from roadway bushes, directly into our path. We veer, skid to a stop. He is young, maybe eighteen or nineteen years old, drunk, staggering, struggling for balance, but keeping his rifle aimed toward us. There is scarcely time to be afraid, just a brief moment before he falls toward the hood of our car and then manages to right himself. Falling close to the car with its engine running seems to somewhat sober him and he stands upright, steps backward, disappears into the bushes. Rudy agrees it is time to speed to the junction.

I am past being able to take my slow, relaxing breaths. Instead I clutch a paper bag, at the ready for any hyperventilation. Rudy has an awareness that haunts us.

"We must've put the gas station man in danger. Was his fear a fear for all three of us?" And a chilling thought: "Will he remember to hide those dollar bills?"

✈

ONCE in West Berlin, we stay in a modern, convenient hotel, one I choose for the bright red carnations in its window boxes. It has been weeks since we have seen flowers in window boxes. We find the Olympic Field where Hitler had to watch Jesse Owens, an African American, take four gold medals. We visit residents at the famed Berlin Zoo, sample international cuisine on the neon-lit *Ku-Damm* Boulevard, and explore *Ka De Wah*, a six-story department store doubling as an ad for capitalism.

Rudy visits a different section of the German Historical Museum each day. I start to question his fixation on the place, and then I remember it is his history he finds there. He is particularly intent that I go with him to see the Kaiser Wilhelm cathedral. Drastically damaged by Allied bombings in the war, it is rebuilt now, but its original spire still rises high. A "from the ashes" story.

As for me, it has been a long summer in Soviet-controlled nations and I lack enthusiasm for a tour of East Berlin, the other side of the Wall. "But we can't go home without seeing the Pergamon Altar," Rudy insists, "and it's just over there," he says, pointing at the Wall. I know I am losing this argument, for after all, the second-century treasure traveled all the way from Greece to meet us.

In one of those rare but lovely compromises in travel, we find a tour company that offers day trips to the cultural highlights of East Berlin. Rudy checks to be sure the Altar and Babylonian walkway are included; I check to be sure this is a licensed company that follows all the rules in East Germany, and has never left a tourist behind.

At Checkpoint Charlie, a watchtower and guardhouse serving as the border crossing, heavily armed soldiers search our bus and passengers. They pass enormous mirrors under the vehicle, look in the restroom, search under our seats. I am confused: do they think people want to smuggle their way *into* East Germany? When time comes to inspect our passports, mine again causes a stir and delays our bus long enough for me to lose a few friends among the passengers. Rudy again has to explain to guards, in his mix of languages, "She looked better before we started this trip, looked like that picture on the passport." And, shaking his head regretfully, man-to-man, "She has gotten older."

SOMETIMES it helps to start at the saddest place and work your way up to the less sad. Fellow passengers are distraught as the bus drives through East Berlin's empty, car-less streets, passes buildings under construction or being restored.

"It's so gray," they say. "Look, nothing's finished here. Where do people shop?" They bridle against the rigid tour structure that the guide outlines. "Eight minutes here, fifteen minutes there, don't wander away from me, don't miss the bus, for sure, don't miss the bus." These sound like liberal guidelines to Rudy and me, but the groans of our tour mates tell us this is their first experience in a tightly controlled land.

When Rudy and I compare it to Czechoslovakia, we find this region more subtly Soviet. If Czechoslovakia now is the dead of winter, East Berlin is very early spring. Life seems to be rising here, with multiple restorations underway and main squares being refurbished, one or two looking nearly now like their pre-war photos. And—the Pergamon Altar enchants.

CHAPTER ELEVEN

HUNGARY
1983
HUNGARY

WE ARE BASKING IN CAPITALISM AND COLOR IN AUSTRIA, preparing to face communism and gray in Hungary. I am weary of Soviet-occupied countries; my eyes get misty looking at bountiful flower boxes on Salzburg windows or at the variety of fresh food filling the stores. I cannot put the somber faces of Prague out of my mind.

Clearly, though, it is Rudy's turn to find his roots. His

birth mother Francesca, an immigrant to America from Budapest, died shortly after his second birthday. He knows little about her country and culture and is anxious to learn. I have promised to go with him, but today at breakfast in our hotel coffee shop I cannot stop myself from trying a compromise.

"A promise is a promise, I know, and we *will* do this trip, but why not next year? We can get rested and come back next summer and stay longer."

He hesitates, but the blue eyes betray disappointment. "Well, a promise is a promise . . . but if you can't do this, that's different."

I don't know what to say. I put my head down and he moves his chair close to mine, putting his arm around me.

"Sure, hon, we can plan to come back next year if you can't do this now. Maybe next year Hungary will be even more open to us . . . but I just worry that next year they could be completely sealed off from the West. What if this is my last chance?"

He is right, of course, about the volatility of the occupied countries, and also about promises.

APPROACHING the crossing into Hungary, we are startled to see the border gate painted in bright red, green, and white stripes. Moments later the gate rises and soldiers look briefly at our passports and visas, waving us into the country. What kind of occupation is this that allows national colors, bright ones at that, on the border gate, and after a brief identity check simply lets us in? Immediately beyond the border, there is evidence of modest entrepreneurship: a simple wooden roadside stand displays small amounts of produce and colorful hand-embroidered blouses. For once I don't have to beg Rudy not to bargain.

"My mother was a seamstress," he reminds me, adding a notable tip to the four-dollar cost of a bag of fruit and a blouse. "I wore her embroidered gowns in my baby pictures."

As we drive away we see what must be the merchant's family, a woman and three children, emerging from a canvas tent behind the stand. He extends his hand to show them our money and they jubilantly hug each other, forming a tight ring. To this day I can see them; to this day I regret not having turned around and bought another blouse.

On our way to Budapest, we take a series of wrong turns and end up in the wrong direction, lost in the Bukk mountain range. Rudy is delighted at the chance to meet rural Hungary. I want only to meet Budapest and my reserved hotel bed. We notice there are few other cars on the road and those few are old, worn models, certainly none as flashy as our little red Ford Fiesta. We get a lot of attention, horns honking and passengers waving. As we drive into a small village seeking directions, a dozen women who must have been sitting all day at their front windows immediately surround the car. Regardless of age, they wear babushkas and are missing front teeth. Yet lacking both teeth and English does not impede communication.

They read our license plate. "Deutschland, Deutschland."

We choose honesty. "No, Americans."

This is even better. "Americans! Americans! Americans!"

Younger women climb up on the car hood to peer down at us through the sunroof; others moisten fingertips and test the car's white stripe for permanence. One has a cousin in Toronto, Canada, America, and begs us to say hello for her. None are proficient in giving directions to lost tourists: when we call out a town name from the map, hands fly in all directions, pointing to "best route."

It takes awhile before Rudy finds a shopkeeper who can interpret a map and before I have my fill of dumpling-like sweet bread. When it is time to leave, we exchange small hugs and hand touches, then drive slowly down a one-way dirt road, looking back to see the women following our car for several meters, waving good-bye until we disappear.

"We had to go all the way to the Bukk Mountains to find someone who likes us," I say.

"But we found them."

We steel ourselves as we enter Budapest, expecting the gray tones of Prague. In truth, much is gray, but much is also Technicolor. The red, green, and white decorates some shops; in window displays, clothing is of varied colors and price ranges; major reconstruction projects signal the city's growth. The streets of Budapest have energy compared to those in Prague, and it seems to me that pedestrians walk more rapidly, shoulders are more often erect, and eyes look at me. Men gather in small groups in late afternoon, talking quietly, but publicly, in the streets, a sight we did not see in Prague. Nearly all we meet speak German, and many speak English.

Following directions from the state tourist agency IBUSZ to the hotel they have reserved for us, we arrive at the entrance to an elegant art nouveau edifice sited at a beautiful bridge and facing the Danube River. There must be some mistake.

Our sense of being imposters grows: for $68 we have a luxurious river-facing suite with working toilet, sumptuous breakfast in the restaurant, and soaking time in any of the two indoor thermal spas, or two outdoor pools, one equipped with a wave machine. In each of these settings we meet tourists and Hungarians alike. We have arrived, but it is rather unsettling. Tourism is clearly a state goal, but which state?

Road weary, we have dinner in the hotel restaurant. Gilded walls, flowers, table lamps, and highly starched tablecloths are the backdrop for attentive, tuxedoed waiters, an orchestra, and a multi-course gourmet meal. Through our stay, we learn these old-world elements are standard even in inexpensive tourist cafes.

Our favorite becomes a Hungarian restaurant located on Lenin Court, famous for its traditional country-style goulash. On our second visit there, Rudy and I are hand in hand descending a staircase into the main dining room when he stops abruptly to listen to the sounds of Liszt.

"It's the violins," he says. "That's what Father told me, 'love happened amidst the strains of violins.'"

His papa as a young man grew enamored with a Hungarian restaurant on 39th Street in New York City, and particularly with a customer, Francesca, a beautiful, dark-haired, dark-eyed woman who sat each night with her elderly husband as admiring violinists circled their table. Over time, Papa attracted the woman's attention and, eventually, her hand in marriage. Divorce in that era was rare, but not surprisingly, Rudy's father was a rule-breaker, and the people of Hungary—we can see even in the midst of Soviet occupation—have a romantic core.

After another day of being lost driving in tangled city streets, I convince Rudy that using cheap taxis will not plunge us into bankruptcy. Better still, the cabs afford a rare opportunity to hear political theories of outspoken drivers. The first driver explains:

"I learn English from friend. Have twelve years school learn Russian. Funny, funny, I not remember Russian."

"What about the children in school?" I ask.

"In school children by compulsion learn Russian. Twelve years. They not remember."

And his story for today: "Reagan, Andropov, and Hungarian president riding in car. Reagan say to driver, 'Turn right here.' Andropov say, 'No, no, turn left here.' Hungarian president say, 'Put turn signal on left and turn right.'"

Driver Two later that day tells of a visitor to Russia who noticed a large map of Europe on the wall. All Soviet bloc countries were in red, the Western countries in white, and Hungary in blue. "That is because Hungary is nothing," the Soviet guide said.

Driver Two also has a brochure for us: a well-known Hungarian folk troupe dances tonight in a nearby auditorium, and he agrees to chauffeur us. As we enter, the audience seems composed of Hungarians (I am learning to differentiate Hungarian women in colorful, loose dresses from Soviet women in dark nylon that sticks in the heat). The first eight rows of seats are roped off, filled rapidly when a busload of Soviet tourists enters.

The lively dancers with their animated faces are more than midway through their program when the mood in the auditorium begins to change. After each number, the Soviet section is clapping and stomping their feet, louder and louder, longer and longer, controlling, dominating the rhythm of the night. The faces of the entertainers tell us this is a frightening, not welcome, reception. Two of the three violinists rise from their chairs to walk behind a side curtain while dancers perform with little energy, eventually taking their bows, pirouetting from the stage and ignoring loud calls for encores.

We learn that Hungary is considered "the happiest barrack" within the eastern bloc. Compared to other occupied countries, and against the odds, Hungary sustains a more liberal economy, press, and artistic world.

Rudy, for one, is happy that his mother's land resists.

Chapter Twelve

RUSSIA 1983 RUSSIA

THE UPS MAN LINGERS ON OUR FRONT PORCH, HIS EYES asking, "You're going to *Russia?*" It is nearly Christmas in 1983, and snow and communism are both in full force there. Yet here on our rural California doorstep are two sturdy boxes from a Finnish airline, each prominently labeled "Russian Tour." I can see that the Finnish guides are taking no chances as I pull from the boxes heavy, wool-lined snow boots and a poster-sized communiqué about emergency visas, frostbite, and hypothermia. In addition to the traction boots, we are directed to wear inner socks and outer socks, inner gloves and outer gloves, furry hats with ear flaps, and silk underwear underneath everything wool.

Two weeks earlier Rudy is reading the Sunday edition of the *San Francisco Chronicle* when a small ad in the travel section has his attention.

Waving the newspaper in front of me, he enthuses, "Look —a three-week, all-expenses-paid trip to Russia for eleven hundred dollars. We can't stay three weeks at the local Motel 6 for that."

I avoid a pedantic argument about how we are not vacationing at the local Motel 6 anytime soon, focusing instead on what I see as the central issue. "But I thought there was a State Department warning, kind of an embargo against Russian travel—you remember, after the downing of that plane."

"Well, that embargo must have gone away. Here's the ad."

THE advisory has in fact gone away. Just as the Korean passenger jet had gone away when it was shot from the sky three months earlier by Russian forces. Piecing together facts and rumors, we come to believe that the tour is among the first sanctioned after the advisory, likely subsidized by a Soviet Union intent on attracting Western dollars.

Obviously, Rudy's *Look for the free lunch* rule is in full

play, but it has company. "Got to put the bucket list in order. There's no time like the present," he says. "In another year they might not let us visit at all."

When friends ask me why I am going for the Christmas season to a country that does not have Christmas, and is cold, I have to admit that once more I am caught up in the tornado that is Rudy.

✈

EVEN we wonder about our fellow travelers—what kind of people would live in San Francisco, not have obligations or invitations for the holidays, answer an ad on a Sunday morning in late November, and two weeks later be heading to Russia? As we survey the group assembled in the airport for our flight, one answer comes to mind: "Very interesting people."

Ingrid is a voluptuous blonde in her late 20s, a Marilyn Monroe-style beauty, who finds it impossible to stow her wardrobe in suitcases. She would, she tells her spectacled companion Jonathan, need to borrow a bit of money to ship her steamer trunk. As Jonathan searches his briefcase for traveler's checks, Henri, a tall, thin, goateed man in a buttery leather jacket, rises quickly from his lady companion's side to offer the beauty a fistful of cash. Airport personnel vie to be Ingrid's luggage inspectors.

Mark, full-figured, full-bearded, and covered in fur, has brought a thin quiet wife and a thin quiet daughter whose windbreaker jackets suggest they were told the destination was Hawaii. Mark is not quiet, sharing highlights of Russian history with anyone seeming to listen. The most attentive member of his small audience is Holly, who, like her teenage daughter, is clad in sandals and cotton. An older gentleman, Neal, dressed in a black suit and lacy, ruffled ivory shirt, introduces his twin, Nick, dressed in a black suit and lacy, ruffled ivory shirt. Five other older couples complete our tour group. They have to this point no distinguishing marks, except that each of the men has served in World War II.

We have not even boarded the plane when I know that Russia itself will have to compete for my attention.

Our overnight stay in a Helsinki hotel is advertised as time to refresh ourselves between the long flight and the next day's bus trip to the Russian border. Outside our window, the snow falls steadily. Inside, Rudy snores his soft relaxed purr, undoubtedly replaying scenes from his beloved movie, *Doctor Zhivago*. Someone, however, needs to stay awake, making emergency plans for potential dramatic events of our own. For starters, I develop strategies that cover the evacuation of the American embassy, theft of our visas, and imprisonment.

I am right. Rudy wakes up early, humming the *Zhivago* theme and calling me Lara.

At breakfast we learn that one of the couples has left our frigid, adventurous tour to fly to sunny, predictable southern Spain. I would campaign for that option too if I didn't know the *Adapt* rule.

The group, minus two, boards a comfortable, warm bus to head northeast within Finland, along the Russian border. Despite our bets to the contrary, everyone appears on time, although Ingrid has many things to say about the "morning rush" and what it does to one's composure and complexion.

The Finnish guide Hanna is a charmer, a short, full-figured, motherly woman who we guess could soften the impact of the trip ahead and make us chicken soup as needed. In her soft voice, she lets us know that we are not taking a shortcut or even a direct route to Moscow; we are expected to cross into Russia at a more remote border.

"This particular border is ready for us," she explains.

There is no way to tease out of her a definition of "ready."

THE group settles in for the long drive, growing quiet as we put our faces firmly to the windows, not unlike schoolchildren, seeing only the whitest of snows, and pondering what it means to be ready for us.

After allowing us some time for what she must have assumed was meditation, Hanna speaks at length of Russian history, her voice catching on some phrases, phrases we do not know now that will decades later define our trip:

"The Russians suffered greatly in their history, in their wars."

"The Finns also suffered. Borders can be difficult."

"There is a difference between people and governments."

Rudy was one of those World War II veterans who had never expected to return home, but who, when he did, began a long study to understand what had happened. When Hanna pauses for a time, he moves to sit beside her. Returning later to his seat next to mine, he bends over, looking down at his hands, and whispers, "Hanna's sister was killed in the war. This is a hard trip for her."

Sometime later the bus slows, turning onto a narrow pathway that leads to a barricade and a long wooden hut sitting off to the left, alone in the snow. Sounds of our engine bring half a dozen soldiers, armed with rifles, to posts along the barricade. One with more medals than the others indicates our bus is to halt and that we are to enter the hut.

Hanna, again in that quiet voice, says, "You will please follow the guards' directions very carefully . . . yes?"

We all nod. I check to be sure Rudy does too.

And so we bundle up to stand in the snowfield, somewhat alphabetically, holding our possessions. Inside the hut five more armed soldiers stand behind a long wooden counter, holding stacks of paper they consult each time a passport and visa are presented. In the meantime, soldiers at the barricade search inside and beneath the bus, under its hood and in its luggage compartments.

Very gradually, the group begins to realize that we are all being cleared for entry. Eyes widen and a few confide to companions, "I can't believe this," or "Who would guess?" Most of us had apparently concluded that our fellow tourists must be C.I.A. agents. Who but a paid employee would be on this trip?

We have a second surprise: as the barricade is lifted, a tall, muscular woman in a dark fur coat and hat, carrying a small black valise, comes from inside the hut and walks stiffly, purposefully, to our bus.

Hanna shakes the woman's hand and turns to us. "This is our Russian Intourist guide. She will in some ways be in charge now."

The woman seems to have questions about the wording of that last sentence. "In some ways?" she repeats loudly. "I am Antonina. I will show you my country." Then she adds,

"Officially the name it is Russian Soviet Federative Socialist Republic, but it is acceptable for you to call it Russia."

I turn to look Rudy straight in the eyes, hoping to forestall any resistance he might possibly have to a highly authoritative woman. In what I admit is a hissing voice, I say, "Promise me you'll keep a low profile and not get into any trouble with this lady."

"I'll try."

Try? I worry about that response.

Within an hour, the smokers on board call for a break, and the bus stops in a rural wooded area where snowy hills are checkered with small, two- or three-room wooden huts. These, Antonina explains, are *dacha,* summer vacation homes reserved for loyal city workers as a reward from a grateful government.

She ignores the question, "Why do all these 'summer homes' have plumes of smoke coming out of their chimneys?"

✈

SEVERAL men in the group follow Rudy's lead, sprinting off up a hill to seek the answer, and to have, as he phrases it later in their defense, "some people-to-people exchange." A small, elderly man inside one of the huts opens his door at the first loud knock, spotting in astonishment a fancy bus parked down the hill and five well-garbed foreigners on his porch. There is standing room only for the visitors, but his wife turns to the wood-burning stove to see how far the stew might stretch.

While Antonina screams below, hurling threats of deportation, the men empty their pockets of gifts of ballpoint pens and coins, taste spoonfuls of stew, admire family photos brought from a closet, and discover that Rudy's childhood German, along with pats on the back, is sufficient to cement new friendship.

Antonina is not to be pacified when the men return to the bus. Through more shrill screams we learn that those who had gone visiting had endangered our trip. Our group must be reported, and we must never leave her side again. Nearly tearful, she tells us she could lose her job and implies that Hanna might also face some sort of unnamed trouble. One by one the men come forward to tell her they are sorry.

The days before Moscow are spent seeing small towns, the nights spent eating simple dinners and sleeping in simple rooms. I, and even Rudy, seem to have made peace with the terms of our travel.

With little to see as the bus drives on in the light snow-falls, we turn for entertainment to what Rudy has labeled "our motley group." Each morning the identical twins in identical clothing claim the same front seats. The teenage girl still in her sandals positions herself close behind the driver where, if she turns just right, she can watch his brown eyes and blond hair in the rearview mirror. In the meantime, her mother, also still in her sandals, moves closer to Mark, the better to follow his daily talks on Russian history. Henri and Ingrid gravitate toward the rear of the bus, leaving their original companions up front to compare notes on Moscow museums. Across the aisle from us, one of the older men shares his life goal: to see every remote village in Siberia and Micronesia.

"Why?" I ask.

"Because they are there."

As I am pondering just how crazy this man is, Rudy shakes his head and says in admiration, "What a guy."

The drama increases as we enter the outskirts of Moscow in search of our hotel. It takes us awhile to realize that the bus is circling the city, rounding the same blocks repeatedly, until an hour, then two, go by. Antonina has not been allowed to carry a city map.

Eventually an answer is found standing on a curb. Antonina suddenly orders our driver to pull over so that she might invite onto the bus a well-decorated military man she calls General. Generals have maps.

✈

AFTER our introduction to Russia in its humbler towns, the Moscow hotel is startling—a glass and chrome high rise, a picture of modern construction that could stand proudly in any American metropolis.

Inside, however, the hotel has amenities that do not remind us of home. We learn at the check-in counter that under no circumstances can we change rooms, as ours has been prepared for us alone. A key monitor sits on each floor, between the stairwell and elevator. She gives us our key to open our door, and we return it to her each time for "safekeeping." A light fixture in each room hangs low and is mysteriously connected to the telephone concierge service—when we talk to each other about how cold the room is, the phone rings and an operator inquires about our number of blankets. In the dining room, a lamp hangs low in the midst of each small table. One can speak below it of a desire for more borscht and, within minutes, have it brought from the kitchen. Each guest room has a small television that broadcasts what we presume is national news, as well as film footage nearly twenty years old of the Los Angeles Watts riots.

Late that first night in Moscow, Rudy beckons me to the window at the end of our hallway, where we can see the city in all its lights spread out below us.

"This is a formidable country, a formidable force," he says quietly.

I startle. Do I hear a measure of fear in his voice?

If it is fear that I hear and fear I share, it begins to fade a bit in both of us. The Russian treasures in Moscow and Leningrad—St. Basil's, the Kremlin, the Hermitage, the Winter Palace, operas and ballets—are simply too beautiful to be obscured by fear.

I am enthralled by the Moscow Circus troupe, but I most remember the popcorn man. Reaching the head of a long line, I hand carefully counted Russian currency to the full-bearded, apron-clad popcorn vendor.

He smiles a bit at the correct change, looks up, and asks, "Amer-i-cain?"

I nod yes and try to smile, aware the people in the long line behind me are leaning forward and have gone quiet.

The man's demeanor shifts and he scowls dramatically. "You, you have Reag-onn. Pres-dent Reag-gon."

I nod again, guiltily.

"We, we have Andropov."

The popcorn man then lifts his two fists, facing them toward each other in mock battle, and raises his voice. "Ugh, ugh on Reag-gon, Ugh on Andropov. No. No."

Fists lowered then, he bursts into a wide smile and extends both arms toward me. "But you. Me. Yes, yes." I stop holding my breath and look behind me. The people in line only stare.

There is no denying that our group misses the Christmas season of home. The Russian white-fur-clad Father Winter is just not enough of a substitute, and the churches turned cold museums offer little comfort.

I answer a soft knock one night at our Moscow hotel room. The middle-aged sturdy woman, our key monitor, stands holding a foot-high thin plastic tree. She hands it to me and points to our suitcases. She wants us to keep the tree. What a time for language to fail us, when we want to protest her generosity, to say the tree should stay with her and her family, to say we love her shy smile when every day she hands us our key. But we know only a simple "thank you," and the way she backs carefully out the door rules out our hugs.

The next day when she hands us our room key, she lowers her eyes, and we fear we have come too close. But that evening she knocks again, and this time her gestures say I should follow her. She leads me to a windowless, gray room one fourth the size of ours, her home. She pulls a footstool from under the narrow bed and indicates I am to climb on it to retrieve a box from the top closet shelf. When I do, I see the box holds a strand of tiny red, white, and green lights. They are for me.

As the days go on, Antonina relaxes her grip on us and Rudy slips through the opening in her vigilance. She carefully avoids looking at his empty seat on the bus, for it means he has gone off in his disguise, speaking basic German, wearing old European shoes, hat, and coat. Rudy has discovered the Moscow subway system and the city is his.

In the evenings, he and I walk through the hotel so that he can tell of the day's adventures without the presence of our room's listening lamp. He speaks of meeting a woman who wants to go with him to America; learning from police that one should not take pictures in a subway station no matter how grand the art; finding the Intourist office staffed by armed forces, not travel agents; and helping the department store clerk replace her abacus with a new credit card machine. Nothing in his travels upsets him except seeing the young, delicate mother in the Russian military museum, proudly showing her three-year-old the arsenal.

IN the Leningrad hotel each night before dinner, Rudy walks slowly past the lobby bar on his way to the tourist dining room. I know it is just a matter of time before he can no longer resist the urge to meet and mingle over evening vodka. He has already visited with hotel janitors in their break room where they start the day with Fanta and vodka. True enough—one evening I find him sitting in the midst of six smartly dressed young Russians.

"Hi, honey. My friends here asked if my jacket is Ralph Lauren and I said it was Goodwill Thrift. They think I'm joking. Their television says all Americans are rich."

I smile one of those tentative little pulls on the lower lip, something perhaps more like a grimace. This does not feel safe.

The three girls take turns opening their bags to show me

the fruits of their shopping tour, one displaying a new warm hat, another pulling out a brown wool sweater, the third showing three boxes of embossed greeting cards depicting the white-fur-clad Father Winter amidst a field of blue and white snowflakes.

The sharing complete, we learn the young couples have secrets to tell. One of the girls, an international telephone operator, knows just enough English to translate in a whisper for her friends.

"America should know. Children here, ten years old, they join Young Pioneers. They are trained to be soldiers. The television up in your room, it shows them marching in the towns."

"The government says homosexuals are mentally ill. They put them in institutions for years, lifetimes."

Her revelations end abruptly when her boyfriend notices three men in long black coats enter the lobby.

"Do not look up," the young man says to Rudy and me. "Go to the bar. You do not know us."

Rudy goes to order a drink while I sit unable to will my legs to movement. The young people head for the outside doors, and the three men do too. As she leaves, one of the girls reaches over me, placing a bag in my lap, saying, "For American lady."

A full ten minutes later, when our new friends are gone, when at last my fingers will move, I open the bag and find the three boxes of Father Winter greeting cards. On each card, Father Winter wears a luxurious white fur coat and hat, and carries an elegant walking stick.

At breakfast on our last morning in Russia, Hanna in that quiet voice tells us that our group has lost members. Ingrid has flown off in the night for Paris with Henri and her steamer trunk. Her departure is likely a relief for Russian commanders, for each time she has alighted our bus, young soldiers have followed her like ducklings.

"To think," Rudy says, "one American blonde very nearly brought down the entire Russian military."

But Hanna says that Ingrid and her new love are not the only group members missing. We learn that earlier that same morning two black-coated men in a gray van had picked up Mark where he waited in the snow on the corner outside the hotel. Mark had apparently defected to Russia.

Hanna reminds us that those who have gone have left behind in our group their family or lovers, and that we are now a community with responsibilities.

We are a somber group boarding our bus in Leningrad for our last event, scheduled to partake in what Antonina describes as our "culminating cultural experience" before leaving on the night train to Finland. There will, she says, be a "roundtable discussion" with Russian civic leaders about international relations and World War II experiences. In our days in Russia, we have grown more and more aware that the war, most especially the brutal siege and blockade of Leningrad at the hands of the German Army, is not in the past here, but very much present. And how could it not be? Our local guides cried telling of frozen winter nights, starvation, agonizing deaths of parents, grandparents, children, all defenseless for over two years, over eight hundred days, in a city cut off from food, medicines, supplies, where flour was mixed in half measure with sawdust to form bread secured by ration cards. There is not a way to forget.

The five veterans in our group look forward to the exchange, to talking of a war when Americans and Russians fought on the same side to defeat the German Army. What our veterans have not reckoned with is that the still-present feelings of abandonment and horror in Leningrad are accompanied by anger and blame. Hanna alone seems frightened.

As we enter the auditorium, we see there is no round table, only metal folding chairs on the floor facing six padded recliners lined up on a stage high above us. Hanna takes a metal chair and moves it far back to the corner of the large room, where she will sit. All of us, our group and those six on the stage, keep bundled up in coats and scarves against the frigid room and atmosphere. A translator comes to the microphone and the speeches begin. The two hours are like twenty—a mix of angry tears, recriminations, pictures of lost loved ones held high. There is such sorrow and anger in the chairs above us as they cry, "America left us, the world left us, left us for years to freeze and die."

But there is also sorrow and anger on the auditorium floor. Our World War II veterans are not invited to speak, but they nonetheless rise one by one, telling of battles they fought, flights they endured, comrades, brothers they lost. America was being wrongly accused, they say. "We did what we could. The war was everywhere."

I hold onto Rudy's hand, silently begging him to stay seated. His hands are always warm, but today they are ice.

He squeezes my hand and whispers, "Don't worry. I'm not adding to this. There's nothing to say to make it better."

The loud voices and outrage continue until, speaking of his years as a prisoner of war, the man who wants now to see villages of Siberia and Micronesia sobs and sobs. It is quiet for what seems a long time, each side replaying its own nightmares. In the end, another of our group, a woman, rises and says the words I want to say but cannot.

"We are so sorry. We are so sorry for all that happened, both sides, to all our men and families. We are so sorry."

There is no response from the men on the stage, only staring eyes.

From within the silence that continues, Hanna stands, and her voice is softer than ever. "It is time to go now. It is time for your train."

We have a hard time rising from our chairs, then moving toward the door. It is as if we are waking slowly from a long and frightening night and stumbling about for balance, balance that eludes us. Our veterans still weep but more and more quietly, the rest of us forming tight, protective rings around each of them.

We drive to the station in a soundless bus and board a heavily guarded train.

Snowfall envelops us as our old, rattling train starts to move away from the dark Leningrad station. In this one way, our trip to Russia ends as it began: as on our first day here, we press our faces against the foggy windows, straining to make sense of bleak landscape. But in many other ways, nothing is the same. We are not the group that entered the country three weeks ago. One of us defected; two ran off to Paris; two others gave up early, lured by a sunny Spanish coast. Those of us who remain are not who we were. We are not the smiling Americans who ran up a hillside to visit a couple in their *dacha*, nor are we the tourists who laughingly called for more soup through the lamp that hung above a café table.

Rudy has spoken little since the afternoon encounter with the Russian veterans. When I ask him how he is feeling, he reaches across for my hand and says, "Later. We'll talk later. It was too much talk today."

I know what he means. When I try to look out the small train window, I see and hear only the six men on the stage today, screaming, unyielding. It takes a long time before those faces begin to blur—and there are others before me: the key lady, the young Russians, my popcorn man.

CHAPTER THIRTEEN

WE ARE, WE HOPE, TRAVELING THROUGH THE DARK NIGHT
from Russia to the Finnish border. Rudy tries to verify our
destination, speaking loudly to the guard outside our compartment. "Finland? We go Finland?" Worse yet, he tries in
Russian. The guard looks more confused and, after several
attempts, Rudy concludes that his handy book of Russian
phrases has failed him again.

Our train compartments are narrow, holding two passengers sitting knee-to-knee, yet tour mates do not gather in the wide, guarded corridor to share stories or souvenirs. Only in the bathroom line do we exchange messages through wide-eyed looks, glances toward guards, fingers crossed. One man in line has a small compass that he pulls from his pocket; showing it to us, his smile says we are in fact traveling in the direction of Helsinki.

"So far, so good," Rudy responds.

He tries to be his usual optimistic self, even though we both know it is a façade designed to keep me from a bout of embarrassing primal screams. "Nothing to worry about, Mare. They're probably glad to get rid of us. We weren't exactly compliant communists."

I see things a little differently. "Think of how much we'd be worth in ransom."

He raises his eyebrows, silently looks at me over his reading glasses, and I concede. "Well, okay, maybe not much."

The night is long, punctuated only by the visits of an elderly, bent-over steward dressed in a worn uniform. The man carries an old wooden tray, every time with the same provisions: a dry ham sandwich to be shared and tea in two glass mugs, each covered with elaborate silver work. The mugs catch Rudy's eye.

"Beautiful," he says, tracing the filigreed silver designs with his fingers. "Very beautiful, sir."

The steward is puzzled, but when Rudy adds a broad smile and holds one of the mugs in a gesture to his heart, the man nods.

In the still-dark early morning, the train slows as if approaching a station or—better yet—a border. We hear each compartment's sliding door being closed tight and locked from the outside. I need a bathroom, and I am not alone. Cries of anguish come from compartments all around us. One by one the doors are unlocked and two guards squeeze into each tiny room, peruse passports and visas, and shine flashlights under benches and behind window coverings.

No, no one extra boarded in Leningrad, spent the night behind our tattered curtain, or shared our ham sandwich. Once assured of our innocence, the guards unlock our door and Rudy lifts our cases down from the overhead rack. Just then our steward quietly enters the compartment carrying a brown paper bag. He gestures for us to look inside and there they are, the two silver mugs. They are going home with us. We know this because he closes the door, then helps Rudy open his case and stuff them between underwear and pajamas. My sense of impending doom rises; I know our treasures will be found by customs. I just don't know which customs.

Rudy gives me a look that says, "Pull it together. We cannot hurt his feelings."

I flash him the "All right, all right" response.

We have each secreted away a few Russian coins and now we pull them out for our benefactor. "*Nyet,*" he says, "*Nyet,*" shaking his head. He places one hand to his heart and gives a small bow as he steps back into the corridor.

The border station is a long wooden structure furnished with rough-hewn benches. A small table is lined with the familiar sandwiches and tea is joined by hot cocoa. My travel companions are jubilant as Finnish agents do a cursory check of passports and cases, then escort each of us across an icy path to a comfortable bus waiting outside, lights and heater blasting against the yet-to-be-sunrise morning.

I do not look happy, our travel companions observe. Don't I realize our journey is over? They are right. I have fought tears since the steward backed out of our compartment. Actually, I have fought tears since I met the key lady.

"IT'S you, it's really you," the teenage girl in sandals screams as she sees that our new bus driver is our earlier bus driver, the one she sadly kissed good-bye two weeks ago when we crossed into Russia. True enough, her Christmas present from the tour company has arrived, and she once again seats herself behind him so that she might view in the mirror those unforgettable brown eyes and tousled blond curls.

Christmas Eve? It can't be. Apparently in the land of Father Winter we lost track of our own holidays. But our guide Hanna stands at the front of the bus, all alone with no Intourist guide, microphone in hand and smiling broadly, telling us, "You have been good. It's time for you to meet Santa Claus."

We look at each other, puzzled until she explains.

"The Finnish Tour Company arranged a surprise for us. We are not going back to the city hotel in Helsinki to wait for tomorrow's flight. We are going where Finnish families go for this special night, to a resort high in the hills above the city. There you will see how Finns celebrate. There you will be part of it. What do you think? Do you want to go with me?"

Unanimous.

The visions of sugarplums dancing now in our heads are nothing compared to the reality of the welcoming, wooden, snow-covered lodge. From a breakfast buffet unlike any we have ever seen—spreading across five long tables—to the young guests dressed in velvet and sitting beneath a massive tree, the resort is something nice children dream of.

The clerk shows us the indoor pool and saunas, tells us that more of the steam baths can be found in wooden sheds outdoors on Santa's trail. "Don't miss it tonight," he says. "There will be dinner and carols indoors, but on Santa's trail there will be surprises. Have you all been good?"

That evening, after a sauna and long, long nap, I leave Rudy slumbering. After putting on all of my clothing to face icy weather, I make a brief circuit of the dining room to be sure I haven't dreamed it, then begin to walk around the side of the hotel. Candlelit lanterns lining the path distract me and I come face to face, rather face to nose, with a live reindeer. He is very nearly my height—and in fact has a reddish nose—and is accompanied by friends.

"Ho, ho, ho," a voice calls out from a large sleigh behind a team of eight or nine of the large creatures.

I don't know what one says to the genuine Santa and manage a feeble "Merry Christmas. Merry Christmas, Santa."

I race to find Rudy in the dining room. "Come with me," I say hurriedly. "This is no shopping mall Santa. That beard is the real deal. And you will not believe the reindeer."

I take him by the hand and we walk along the path . . .

and walk along the path. No Santa. No reindeer. Rudy is giving me that concerned look he gives me when I have bumped my head.

There may not be Santa, sleigh, and reindeer, but the candlelit path leads up the snowy hills to a series of saunas and warming huts. Inside each hut, women dressed head-to-toe in fur stir big cast-iron pots over the fire. Cups of mulled wine smell of cardamom and cinnamon. We have a choice for warming soup—reindeer stew or vegetable broth. Rudy tries a spoonful of reindeer stew. I, however, cannot, now that I have had a recent personal relationship with one.

We visit each of the six huts, walking uphill to the end of the trail, then start down. The team of reindeer and magnificent sleigh are in front of the lodge, patiently waiting to continue their night of flying and gifting. In the dining room, the sounds and smells of Christmas preside. Santa is on a throne, with children waiting in line to sit on the famous lap. I may be imagining this—I do that sometimes—but I am almost certain that, as he left, his last wink was for me.

THE next morning, Christmas Day, just in time for our airport departure, bellhops come for our luggage. But when they bring our cases to the bus, the luggage compartments are still locked. So is the bus itself. No heater runs to spare us morning ice; no windows are defrosted; no driver is in sight. Hanna looks worriedly at her watch and counts her passengers. One is missing: a teenage girl who wears sandals in the snow. Departure time comes and goes while Hanna confronts the teen's mother.

"Madam, what is your daughter's room number? No, madam, we do not have time to be discreet. Madam, give me her room key."

CHAPTER FOURTEEN

EGYPT
1984
EGYPT

"SOMETHING'S WRONG," RUDY SAYS. "THIS PLANE ISN'T taking off. We're taxiing back to the Cairo terminal."

Leaning across him to look out the window, I have to agree. Something is wrong when a dozen soldiers dressed in camouflage and with assault rifles at the ready advance on the tarmac toward our plane, and the stewardess unlatches the cabin door. Our usually talkative tour companions fall silent, reaching for passports and each other. We sit as still as we can as soldiers move slowly down the aisle, pausing at every row to look each of us in the eye.

Rudy takes my hand and risks a whisper. "Try to relax, hon. Take those deep breaths you take."

I can't remember how I do those. The soldiers walk past our row, stopping just behind us to remove at gunpoint two of our group members. We hear only one English word as the pair is escorted up the aisle and out the door: "prison."

We had seen soldiers earlier when they ringed our airport boarding area, watching us intently as we waited for our plane to Aswan. The thoroughness of Cairo airport security shocked us, for in 1984 Egypt was already living on the edge of what we would one day call terrorism. We learn what has been left out of the travel brochures—Egyptian government officials and tourists are both popular targets. In American airports, we had come to expect more casual surveys, at most passing through a metal detector portal, while our carry-on luggage is X-rayed. Here in Cairo, armed guards direct us through three portals, open and X-ray our luggage multiple times, restrict our group to a small, guarded waiting area, and analyze our passports for earlier travel to enemy territories. Seat assignments seem a particular concern, and in several cases, our assigned seats are shuffled and families or companions separated.

This is why our two tour members go to prison that day: unlike the long-married couples in the group, this unmarried pair could not bear being separated for the hour-long flight.

"No," the man says simply as the stewardess shows him his assigned seat across the aisle.

"No?" she checks her understanding. "You will not be in your seat?"

"I will not."

She tries once more. "You will not?"

"I will not."

When the soldiers disembark with the loving couple, every passenger has an opinion. Most agree it is good to see Egypt guarding its security and order, its priceless heritage. All agree that this is the couple we would have chosen if there had been a "who will get removed" lottery. None of us can stop wondering just what it is the Egyptians are expecting to happen.

Our guide Amun confers with the pilot and stewardesses before telling us that our flight will now proceed and that we will be respectful of the flight crew's authority. No arguments there.

This day has not begun easily, but this guide has won Rudy's favor. Rudy has a rule that says one must rise before dawn to see popular places before popular times. Amun wants us to see the temple at Abu Simbel near Aswan with the first rays of sun shining directly on the statues, well before any other tourist group reaches the remote location. Rudy and Amun are a match made in heaven.

Amun has roused us at two a.m. this morning, served Nescafé in the lobby, and sent us out the front hotel doors to the coach waiting to take us to the airport. However, there is no coach waiting and the hotel manager is yelling and gesturing wildly, indicating Amun should come to the telephone. Our bus driver has been arrested, our bus confiscated. There is no time for worrying about the bus or the unfortunate driver. We are on our way to sunrise at the temple.

Amun enlists the hotel drivers and calls every taxi company in a twenty-mile radius to get us to our flight. This is the drama drivers dream of: pushing us and our luggage into tiny cars until we can fit no more, setting off in the darkness with lights flashing and horns honking, passing each other in the quest to win the race and get the major tips.

Our driver knows a little English. "I help Americans," he says. "I number one get to airport."

In fact he is number two, and that is enough. As we pull up to the terminal, Rudy is just finishing his twenty-minute lecture on the significance of Abu Simbel, delivered when a woman sitting on the gearbox asks innocently if anyone knows where it is we are going.

It is true: the statues at Abu Simbel would be beautiful in any light, but at sunrise they are magnificent. Our group is alone there as the sun strikes each statue, bathing it in a red, then golden glow. Later that day, when we board a simple, well-worn riverboat for our journey on the Nile, we realize it is time to toast sunset.

After a week of belly dancing shows, rides on camels (they do spit), and toilet repairs, we have bonded with the tour group and our charming crew. Ordinarily Rudy would be "champing at the bit," as he liked to say, anxious to head off on his own to find treasures. I think the examples we have seen of military authority and our reliance on Amun to negotiate hard travel have mellowed my spouse. Only once do he and I collide.

At a very small village, our boat ties up next to a shaky

wharf and we, with plenty of assistance, disembark. Rudy discovers a large outdoor market—in particular he discovers tablecloths made of coarse brownish fabric, embellished with fading stamps of Egyptian pyramids and royalty. There is no label on the wares; if there were, it would explain they were wrinkle guaranteed and color non-fast. Rudy selects one twenty-two feet long.

"It'll look great on our dining room table. Bring back memories, you know?"

"But our dining room table is seven feet long."

"Oh." He thinks. "We can fold it." He sees this is not a winning concept and tries again. "We can cut it up and give parts to our friends."

"Well, I'm sure they'd be overwhelmed, Rude."

The merchant overhears us and joins the discussion. Surprisingly, he has a deal for Meester Rude and the lady. The dramatic bargaining begins and I come to grips with reality: this twenty-two-foot tablecloth will be living at our house. It is exempt from Rudy's rule against large souvenirs. The most I can hope for is that my husband can tear himself away from the sport of bargaining in time to get on our boat before it departs.

I am right to worry about that. I should also have worried about the twenty-two napkins that, according to both Rudy and the merchant, could not be separated from their tablecloth.

"What do you mean they can't be separated?" I ask in a grim tone. "These are not newborn kittens looking for mother."

In the end, Rudy accepts a deal on the large cloth, rejects

a deal on the napkins, and reaches our boat just in time for sailing. The merchant also makes it to the boat in time. He leaps over the watery gap between wharf and vessel, holding the napkins aloft in a plastic bag, and calls out "Meester Rude, Meester Rude" as he runs through the upper deck. I go to our cabin for a nap while our captain and crewmen pull back to the dock to apprehend and disembark their stowaway. And the twenty-two napkins.

We have compromised Rudy's independent travel mandate—his rule against group touring—and now face the consequences. We have grown attached to Amun and this group of Americans. It is early morning Christmas Eve and while they are flying home, Rudy and I are staying behind in Luxor to see more of the Valley of the Kings and the temples north of town. This trip is a childhood dream fulfilled for Rudy, and he is not about to leave the antiquities behind after just a short group tour.

"I'll remember you every time I sit at a tablecloth," one woman tells Rudy.

"I'll just keep praying for you," another says to me.

I try to reassure our new friends, fingers crossed. "Don't worry about us. We'll be just fine here . . . alone . . . at Christmas . . . the only ones celebrating Christmas here in a non-Christian country . . . alone."

✈

I realize that we have had experiences with these people that make us all a bit somber and leave me wanting to go home with any one of them, maybe the lady from Nebraska or the couple from Arkansas. We stand in the dirt street, suitcases at our feet, waving good-bye as the tour bus pulls away. The hotel is directly behind us, and as the bus leaves, two bellmen come to help with luggage. The hotel has no special lights, no décor suggesting this might be a holiday. The bellmen don't smile, but they seem efficient, helpful. What more do we need? We need our busload of tour members, that's what we need. Rudy reminds me we have been in a cocoon, sheltered from meeting Egyptians, and that these days ahead are our chance to learn.

When we realize there is no public bus to the remote northern temples, we look for a driver for the day. The hotel manager highly recommends Rashidi. From what we can understand, Rashidi has references, recommendations from Americans, even some from California. Amazingly, this experienced driver and his experienced Plymouth are very inexpensive. Rudy signs us up.

Rudy and I are trying to close our car doors and locate missing seat belts when Rashidi speeds out of the driveway, darting around wagons, donkeys, merchant stands, and pedestrians, reaching at last a one-lane, unpaved open road where the car can show its true power. With one hand lightly on the steering wheel, Rashidi stretches out, reaches into the open glove compartment, and pulls out a thick stack of letters that he hands to Rudy.

"Theese Ameri-cain. What you say, recommends."

Rudy shuffles through the letters, apparently sorting them by rating.

I protest. "Hey, are you censoring those?"

"Well," he admits, handing them over, "they're all about the same."

In fact, these were letters left for us by fellow Americans who had gone before us and cared about us.

"You will never have a faster ride to the temples."

"We're race car fans, but this beats that."

"Just close your eyes. Good luck."

"If you think the ride going to the temple is terrifying, wait until the ride home."

Rudy is not one to ignore information. He successfully conveys to Rashidi that we will pay more for more hours, for a slower ride, so that we can see the land. As it turns out, Rashidi is not merely a driver; he transforms into a tour guide who proudly shows us each camel, petrol station, and banana plant along the stark back roads. The poverty in the villages is far more pervasive than we saw last week on our group tour. This is not yet an area profiting from tourism—there are few other visitors, and no souvenir shops or food stands.

The temples sit out in the desert nearly alone today, Dendera honoring Hathor, goddess of love and joy, Abydos with its preserved bas-reliefs holding the Lord of the Underworld. With the tour group, we would have been here a few minutes at most, for despite their elegance, these are, in tourist literature, considered "lesser" structures. Ordinarily the heat of the day would have made us yearn for an air-conditioned bus, but the goddess of love and joy and her Lord of the Underworld distract us.

Our visit complete, we leave to go back to our hotel. Starting out on the main but narrow dirt road, we come upon a scene of mourning—a cow, hit by a car or truck, lying on the road. Men, women, and children walk from all directions to kneel at its side. Perhaps twenty are here now, encircling the animal, and we can see more in the distance, making their journey.

Rashidi pulls over to pay respects to the family and the cow, saying in a few English words that the animal was all the family had and the village was sad for them. He cries, embracing an older woman standing closest to the cow. We stand far back on the edge of the mourners, keeping our heads bowed. When Rashidi returns to us, we show him the coins we have. He selects only one and takes it to the woman.

OUR ride home is slow and subdued.

That evening the headwaiter shows us to the only table for two in the dining room, positioned in a dark, distant corner. As we eat silently, sadly, remembering the day and the village and our tour friends, we see the waiters pointing toward us, looking worried, conferring with the manager and with Rashidi.

The next morning, Christmas Day, we come downstairs for breakfast and know which is our table. In the center of the dining room, under its chandelier, sits the table for two, and on it a rangy little bush encircled by a strand of colorful beads and topped with a paper star.

Chapter Fifteen

NEW

1988

ZEALAND

IT IS TRUE WHAT THEY SAY ABOUT NEW ZEALANDERS. WE step off the early-morning flight into a still-dark Auckland, more luggage than usual surrounding us at the airport curb. We plan to camp our way through the islands; Rudy has read about that style of touring here and is sold. I have insisted on a first-night stay in a real downtown hotel, but van after van passes us by, none from our hotel. At last one driver stops.

"I don't go to that hotel," he says, "but you look tired. I'll make a detour."

At the hotel, the desk clerk makes a few phone calls, then tells us we need not sleep in the lobby until check-in time. At six a.m., a room is ready for us. I nap, but restlessly. I have a premonition that this will be my last comfortable bed for four weeks.

THE tired cab-over Daihatsu truck stands pitifully alone in the Auckland rental yard. I have been the last one chosen for sports teams all my life so I know the feeling, but it is hard to be empathetic with this aged, dingy gray camper. My questions come fast.

"We're going to travel in this—this *thing*—for a month?"

"Where's the shower?"

"Is that a toilet seat in the closet?"

"And about the upholstery—just how old is it?"

Rudy offers some defense. "Well, I have to say the description the agency gave doesn't quite match Duke Daihatsu here, but he was the cheapest and now he's the only one left."

He has christened the traffic-beaten old thing, naming it Duke, undeniably beginning the bonding process, and I know where we will sleep this month. I settle for small improvements: a brake check, clean linens, slipcovers for seats and mattress. I also make a bargain, that we will play cribbage each night and after three wins, the loser will do dishes and the victor will decide our entire next day of touring. I do very well at cribbage.

Our maiden voyage is north to the Bay of Islands. We

have not realized, however, that to reach the rural haven we must drive, in the unfamiliar left lane, straight through congested, narrow streets of downtown Auckland. Neither have we realized that Duke has large collapsible mirrors on all sides, and that, since we did not collapse them, they tend to rub up against the sides of passing trucks. There is no easy way to pull over on this road. While Rudy navigates stop-and-go traffic, I take advantage of the pauses to tackle the mirrors, all the while guarding limbs of my own. Our next experience with the legendarily polite New Zealanders is that truck drivers help me without a sarcastic word.

The urban landscape changes within an hour to bucolic hills of brilliant, almost chartreuse, green, lambs dotting the mounds in a pattern not unlike my favorite dotted-swiss dress of childhood. Things are looking up.

IT is time for our relaxing first night as campers in the renowned New Zealand car parks. The campground has all the amenities Rudy has read about—electricity, hot water, showers, fully equipped communal kitchen, recreation room, and snack bar. All closed. We are totally alone. Only two tall street lamps give hints of light. It may be July but it is winter in New Zealand and, although we have read of their mild seasons, it could be that New Zealanders know better.

I never leave home without a flashlight, emergency water, and protein bars, and that is good. We lock the camper door over and over, make the bed, don wool hats, and add two more layers of sweaters before snuggling in for a lonely, cold night. Even Rudy admits our "Meet the People in Their

Campgrounds" itinerary may be in jeopardy. Time will tell.

Time does tell. Nine out of ten accommodations repeat the first night's amenities and solitude, but we learn to ensure that an electrical source is available and that we can take off our wool hats at breakfast. One out of ten accommodations is at least half open if you look at the world as Rudy does, or half shuttered if you see things as I do.

One of these one-in-ten facilities is the grassy backyard of an elderly woman. It is late, dark, and no time to argue about the description she has entered in the Tourist Bureau registry. We have learned by now not to count on a shower, but we do rely on at least one light standard and an electrical plug. Not here.

In another one-in-ten open facility, we encounter a camp manager, taxi and tour driver, postal officer, and wildlife expert. All the same gentleman. He wears special embroidered caps for each role and hands us a variety of his neatly printed business cards.

Wearing his "Preserve New Zealand" cap as we check in, he asks, "Have you ever heard the nocturnal calls of the kiwi?"

"I don't believe we have," I say, making a fatal faux pas.

The next morning Rudy comes back happily from the showers, his merry whistle slowing when he opens the camper door and finds me in my pajamas, boiling water in the microwave while the wildlife expert sits on the only chair, playing a tape recorder. Sounds of the nocturnal kiwi.

To his credit, Rudy is more enchanted than appalled.

I explain later. "He knocked once on the door and walked right in, asking if he had missed morning tea and had I missed the night calls. You have to admit he's friendly, even charming."

"I do."

The gods are with us until they are not. We tour the two islands, relishing clear bright skies in the midst of their winter, checking off each must-see attraction. Even the ferry crossing between islands is calm, pleasant. But one day we drive too far as we head for the campground of the Franz Joseph glacier. Duke complains for the last of the four-hundred-kilometer route, groaning as if he knows something we do not. What we do not know is that the skies are about to open. I have never seen—or felt—so much rain come down in such a short time. I step from the truck cab and someone pours a bucket of cold water over my head. Or at least it seems that way. In the time it takes me to climb back in the cab, a deep mud hole emerges and claims my right foot.

Back in Duke, I peer out and see a neon "Welcome" sign for a lodge next door. "Victory—a hotel," I yell to Rudy, who has disappeared.

His voice comes from afar. "I can't find any power-point outlet," he shouts. "And the lavs are all locked up."

"There's a hotel next door."

"A hotel? Why would we need one of those? We just need a manager to turn on the power."

It does not take long to conclude that the manager is a sane man, home by his fireplace. Or perhaps he is at the hotel. "We can go find him," I say.

The hotel clerk looks at us with a mix of sympathy and amusement. The man wants power turned on in a flooded campground; the wife wants a deluxe room with bathtub. "Room 115," she says. "It will be perfect for you."

In the hotel restaurant, we find a table next to the fireplace for our first dinner out in weeks. I try to forget what we look like in camper clothes. Four bubbly baths later, two for each of us, we sleep in silky splendor. I have forgotten our mission here, but Rudy cannot forget the unseen glaciers. A weather report on television forecasts gloomy skies for four days, gloomy enough to obscure any mountain or glacier, gloomy enough to depress even my mate.

"Think of how far we've come to see these glaciers and now they're hidden," he says.

But when we wake the next morning and pull open the drapes, there it is, bathed in sunlight and snow, a glacier, right outside the window of Room 115.

Chapter Sixteen

THAILAND
1990
THAILAND

I SHOULD HAVE SEEN THIS COMING. AT HOME, IN THE WEEKS before we leave for Thailand, our roof leaks, our heater fails, and two appliances groan in the throes of sudden death. Rudy, always a thrifty—indeed cheap—tourist is in budgetary overdrive even before we leave our driveway. His speech is rapid, anxious.

"We need to cut corners: cheap hotels, picnics in our room, local buses, walking . . . a lot of walking."

Silently asking myself how this would be different from any other trip we have taken in the last fifteen years, I try to pacify him. "Sure. You just keep an eye open for bargains."

What was I thinking?

As we land in the early morning at Chiang Mai airport in mountainous northern Thailand, a throng of drivers stands ready to whisk tourists to their hotels. They hold signs, "Cheap ride," "Hotel 70 baht," calling out prices that decline in moments, stowing luggage in car trunks before visitors can reconsider. The airport lobby empties as our fellow travelers disappear, each in a small, shiny yellow car. Dragging our luggage down the block, we find an aged brown bus, packed with uniformed airport workers apparently heading home to their neighborhoods. They nod and smile, making room for us and our suitcases on the wooden benches.

"We save twenty baht, and we get to see the whole town too," Rudy enthuses during the two-hour bus ride.

Math was never Rudy's best subject; this is not the time to tell him a baht is roughly four cents.

Chiang Mai is one of those places that seduce you gradually. Our first impression is that the air is polluted, the streets congested with *colectivos* and endless streams of motorized rickshaws.

"I thought you read that this is Thailand's artistic center," Rudy says.

But he is the first to convert. While I unpack, he finds street merchants setting up the night market. He is in heaven. There are five-dollar silk robes, ten-dollar fishing vests, bargain jeans and cotton shirts, craft booths everywhere.

He also finds the Whole Earth Restaurant, upstairs above the transcendental meditation center.

"The place is an oasis. Wait until you meet the little shoe boy."

It is true. The child, perhaps six or seven years old, removes our sandals, guards them through our meal, knows which are ours, pulls them on our feet.

No, he does not take a tip. "I help," he says.

Rudy has another reason to visit the night market each evening: we watch native diners and see that the little boy can be thanked in cookies.

✈

IT is one thing to find a cheap bus ride. It is an entirely different thing to find a cheap elephant ride. After a deceptively relaxing day spent exploring handicraft studios and orchid farms, and visiting enormous but gentle-looking elephants, Rudy spies a sign advertising "Special 50% last elephant ride." We have seen the smiling tourists dismounting from Raj-style baskets atop placid elephants in the circus-like ring, having their pictures taken hugging the animal and the pleasant handler, the *mahout*. This touches Rudy, and some sort of childhood dream à la Kipling resurfaces. Besides, there is a fifty percent discount for the last ride of the day. As well there should be.

We learn too late that the last ride of the day is not another tour of the level, circular path, but a return of the tired, hungry elephant to his food and bed at the bottom of a long, steep, wooded cliff. By the time we understand this, it is too late: the four-ton animal has knelt down and we have awkwardly climbed into the royal basket atop him. After he rises slowly and reaches full height, I realize I am nine or ten feet off the ground and there is no seat belt, no restraint, no way to keep from plunging out of the basket. When I protest my seating arrangement, the handlers gesture to the elephant's head. Would the lady like to sit there? I change my cry to "I want off. Now," but it is too late.

Closing up the tourist area for the night, the manager gestures to a slim young *mahout* to accompany us "down." I have taught adolescents and know the signs of a bored, diffident teenager. This one is classic: stuffing a pack of cigarettes in a back pocket, he slouches toward us, dismissing the manager with what must be the Thai equivalent of "yeah, yeah, I got this." Our continued pleas to dismount go unheard as the animal begins his downward trek. Until now, Rudy has been happily taking pictures of our new ride, but at this moment, with the elephant moving out of the ring and heading for the edge of the jungle, Rudy stows the camera and locks arms with me, our white knuckles grasping the edges of the basket. His grip is hard; I rarely feel fear in Rudy, but today is one of those days.

There is a visible trail, presumably worn by elephants moving between the performance arena and the camp far below, but our elephant knows a more interesting route. His choice takes nearly two very long hours, featuring forty- and fifty-degree angles, tasty tree limbs at our eye level, cavernous mud holes, and a fast-running stream. Periodically the *mahout* takes a break, wandering off for toileting, bathing, or smoking, leaving us alone and out of sight atop the massive animal, who enjoys a little free wandering time of his own. With no resistant teenager to plead with or cry to, I have time for a little planning.

"I think our wills are in order, don't you? How about hospitals? Does Chiang Mai have its own or do we fly to Bangkok? That could be bad too. What kind of airplanes do they have?"

Rudy has a suggestion. "Why don't you do those deep breaths you do when you get nervous?"

"Nervous does not begin to describe this."

We agree that if we survive we will lead better lives.

Rudy shows unusual insight. "I don't suppose we should be glad we got the discount."

At last the land levels out and we spot the elephant camp. So does our elephant. It is as if the dinner bell has sounded: his ears rise and he picks up speed, leaving the *mahout* behind, and in record time, lumbering past competing elephants, takes us directly to the food troughs.

A half dozen other *mahouts* encircle us, coaxing the elephant to kneel, bribing it with feed, and finally, helping us dismount onto stepladders. One of the guides knows a bit of English. "Elephant ride tomorrow," he smiles, pointing up the hill.

We carry remnants of the elephant ride with us this week, arms and shoulders stiff from clinging to the basket, leg muscles sore from steadying our bodies, minds tired from graphic memories. Typically, when I have had a trying experience, I allow plenty of time to sit alone and suck my thumb, replaying the event over and over until I tire of it. Rudy, as we have noted, is different.

"Vacation time is running out," he says. "We need to see Chiang Rai, so we'll just have to postpone feeling bad until we get home. I'll go back to the temple—maybe free another bird."

ONE week earlier, on the day we had first arrived in Thailand, Rudy followed the advice of a monk he met at a small temple. He purchased a bird in a metal cage, made a wish, and set it free. Devout Buddhists free birds on their birthdays to make merit, or, in illness, to ask for prolonged life. The monk, however, had assured Rudy that other, less noble wishes are granted daily. As the tiny bird flew away, Rudy was rightfully certain that he would at night market that evening find the fishing vest of his dreams, one with at least ten pockets. The next morning, dressed in his new vest, Rudy discovered his camera was broken. Back to the temple. Another grateful bird. Camera repaired.

Today he is confident. "I'll ask the Buddha for a safe trip to Chiang Rai."

It is good that he freed the bird and petitioned our longer lives; I shudder to think of what our tour would have been like if the little bird had not been involved. As it is, my feeling-sorry-for-myself ritual distracts me, and Rudy, left on his own, finds a bargain-rate driver and tour guide for the four-hour drive north. The pair are grandchild and grandparent—or more likely great-grandparent—she about fifteen, he probably eighty. The age of the car is somewhere in between, measured by the tired springs of the backseat. Our driver is hard of hearing and sleepy; our adolescent guide sits up front, poised to yell into his right ear and/or steady the wheel during drowsy periods. Neither speaks more than a few words of English.

Closing my eyes as the old car speeds to Chiang Rai, I know I have done it again: I have not left Rudy's bargain tour in time to save myself. Now on this deserted road, as in the jungle, there is no easy escape, no small roadside business with a phone booth, no police to rescue tourists realizing too late that theirs is not the luxury package. Even Rudy pales as the driver weaves between the two lanes and their deep potholes, tolerating no one in his way.

We stop at villages not named as models in Fodor's guide. Each is distinct and in each we are the only outsiders, gaining admission by a single coin offered by our teen guide. In normal times, I would be afraid to be alone in these areas, but relief at being out of the car outweighs fear of being kidnapped. In a Karen tribe settlement on flat, open land, old men sleep in dirt-floored opium huts while women cook game over open fire, weave garments, and care for children. The young men, our guide explains, have left to find jobs, usually as *mahouts* in elephant camps.

Other villages cling to steep hills covered with thick vegetation, palm and teak trees, ferns and flowers. The beloved Thai king himself sponsors a floral industry here as an alternative to opium trade. In the Aka tribal area, we pass through a gate to purify our spirits as strangers before the women and children swarm about us, don colorful headdresses, take us by the hand to see their huts, sing and dance. The Yao tribe is a contrast: their village more sophisticated, quiet and orderly. Noted for linguistic skills, they speak several dialects and act as translators between tribes. There is no dancing or singing for tourists here; instead, clusters of women and children gather to embroider and speak quietly together, occasionally pausing to nod shyly at us.

At last the car tour is over, leaving us at a simple Rudy's-pick hotel. On our own again, tuk-tuks and small longboats take us through the Golden Triangle where Laotian and Burmese borders meet Thailand. The Opium Museum displays pictures of drug dens, labeling them "historical photos." The King's sister is in town to open an extravagant, traditionally designed resort. Cannons fire and hundreds of balloons fly in tribute. We are walking toward the public entrance to join the luncheon line when we realize that we are the only pair in shabby jeans and tops, not brilliant silk fabrics. The contrast between the huts we have seen in the villages and the elegant new hotel startles us, turning us back to find a street vendor who has lunch ready, and no dress code.

SHORTLY before we had left home for this trip, a friend told Rudy about Ko Samui. "You can't miss it," he said, "it is the loveliest island in all of Asia." Flying in at dark in the harsh rain, we see hints of that loveliness at the small open-air airport, with its thatched pergola roofs, seats carved from precious woods, airport hostesses in bright embroidered gowns. Riding in the old bus to the remote hotel Rudy has reserved, it becomes harder to see the beauty through the rain. And then there is the hotel, which seems to be a bar—a very local smoke-filled bar—not commonly found in resorts anywhere in the world. Thai patrons, all male, are having a wonderful time, laughing, singing, slapping each other on the back as people do who have been together a long time at a bar. They are welcoming, raising bottles of native beer in honor of the two Americans who stumble into their revelry.

This is not promising, but it is late and dark and stormy. We look around for a registration desk. No sign. We look around for someone who seems to work here. No sign. At last an older woman comes from behind a curtain at the bar and looks at us, puzzled. She explains the situation fully, in Thai. A customer knows just enough English to tell us that someday there will be a hotel here. They will build one. And the tourist information Rudy saw about the hotel?

"Yes, is hotel. Coming."

Sensing that this is no time for an argument, either with the men or with me, Rudy takes the fall. "Maybe I read the ad wrong. I'm not great with details."

Unlike the hotel, the rainstorm is here now, getting louder and interrupting the joy at the bar. The woman confers with her patrons and yes, there is a simple solution: we will sleep in her bed. She pulls the bar curtain back and—voilà!—a small couch made into a twin bed and topped with a light velvet cover. Before we can demur, customers are cheering, offering us bottles of beer for the next toast, getting louder and louder. It is clear they will be here a long, long time tonight.

Somehow Rudy conveys a complex message: we are grateful to the woman, we cannot take her bed from her, and we must get to town. The patrons confer, then select one thin, rather quiet young man, who will take us in his new truck to find a hotel. One that is here now. We three squash into the cab of the older-model Ford, driving over muddy roads until we come to a resort area. The first sign I see announces Ko Samui's "finest new luxury international hotel."

"Stop, stop," I yell. "This is our place."

I know Rudy is grasping his wallet but I am unmoved. I know I may be eating rice all week but I cannot care. We have arrived. I begin what millions of Americans would term a "vacation." My schedule is rigid: up before the breakfast buffet closes at eleven o'clock, swim, walk the beach, lunch before the lunch buffet closes at three o'clock, nap, read, finish drinks and dinner before the candlelit restaurant closes at midnight. Rudy, surprisingly, spends some time relaxing and eating with me, in between his language and flower arranging lessons.

✈

AS we pack for our flight to Bangkok, Rudy begins to tell me about the hotel he has booked.

"It's a real deal, hon."

"Cancel it."

"Cancel it?"

"Cancel it. I have something else in mind."

A few hours later our airport taxi (yes, taxi—I have also chosen the transportation) reaches an American chain hotel, the one with extravagant rooms overlooking River Chao Priya. This is what Rudy has feared, that a week at Ko Samui's top hotel has corrupted me.

This hotel, however, has something for everyone—a massage for me and a twenty-cent boat pass for Rudy. I join him on a river excursion to the Royal Palace, with its massive Emerald Buddha and Reclining Buddha, and visions of brilliant gold leaf, spires, cloisonné, and enamels—artistry that overwhelms us. At one temple I donate coins and the monk offers me an amulet, a gift of good luck, with the image of Buddha engraved in light metal and strung on a beaded chain. I slip it on rapidly. One never knows when one will need extra protection. In the meantime, Rudy sets two birds free to thank the Buddha for taking care of us thus far. We think we have all bases covered, but touring downtown Rudy realizes we have left a stone unturned.

In the center of bustling, chaotic, commercial Bangkok, the Erawan Hotel site is under construction again, this time destined to become a luxury hotel with an adjacent, essential Hindu shrine. In the 1950s, the Thais tell us, hotel construction at this site became a series of nightmares: workers suffering critical injuries, cost overruns delaying the project, a shipload of Italian marble ending at the bottom of the sea instead of the hotel lobby. An astrologer employed by the government to divine the situation concluded that the bad karma began when an unfavorable date was chosen for laying the foundations. Clearly, the only remedy was to erect a Hindu shrine countering the negative forces. As the building of the shrine began, the hotel construction proceeded peacefully.

The Erawan shrine, we note today, is no ordinary shrine. The Brahma and his good spirits are entertained as well as appeased. Dancing girls perform around the clock, a large elephant greets visitors, and trays of fresh food and floral offerings adorn the entry. We hear two explanations for the pile of pornographic magazines in a back corner: in one version, the night guards need something to read, and in another, the good spirits themselves enjoy the collection.

Normally, Rudy at home in California is by no means a religious person, and certainly not a superstitious soul. I am startled at his conversion in Thailand. He has set several birds free over the past few days, dispatching them for a variety of good works—retrieving a lost wallet, helping his tummy digest a challenging meal, bringing world peace. I am getting used to this new man and rather like him. As a sign of that affection, I never share my suspicion that, somewhere down the road or up behind the hill, there is a man with a large cage catching Rudy's birds and returning them for another paid flight.

As we leave the Erawan, Rudy knows what we must do. "We have to think of the future. We need to take a spirit house home with us."

We have seen spirit houses outside most homes and businesses throughout Thailand. A miniature temple mounted on a pillar, each features a replica of a Buddha or Brahman, plus a variety of objects designed to appease the spirits—armor, food, candles, flowers, and plastic animals. In return for a furnished home in a desirable location (preferably amongst large trees), the spirits offer protection to a place and its residents.

But Rudy has a rule about souvenirs and today it is making sense to me. In his edict, souvenirs are confined to small, lightweight objects such as earrings, Christmas ornaments, and scarves. Anything bigger or heavier is banned. I am confused about how the spirit house fits the small, lightweight definition.

"Just exactly how does this spirit house get home?"

"Don't worry. It'll sit on my lap."

"For about twenty hours, the little house sits on your lap?"

"Well, it can't go in cargo."

"Even wrapped up well and crated, it can't go in cargo?"

"I don't think that would be right. It's like I'm entrusted with something."

We fly toward San Francisco, our connecting city, the spirit house with its resident Buddha safely covered and sitting on Rudy's lap. The stewardess serves my meals on my tray, then Rudy's on my tray. It works.

Rudy carries the Buddha and its house through American customs, lifting its cover so the agent might admire the carving. The officer looks a little curious, but not curious enough to spend a lengthy night hearing Rudy's explanation. He shrugs his shoulders and points to the domestic terminal where we will catch a small plane to take us home to Northern California's agricultural valley.

We wait in the crowded lobby, the spirit house on Rudy's lap. Among our fellow passengers is a family of six dressed in embroidered brown wool jackets, pants, and cloth slippers, each clutching a small plastic bag. Every so often one of the children sits on the floor and dumps the contents out, the better to inspect each item. There is a toothbrush, sample-sized toothpaste, a comb, one pair of white socks, a nightshirt. The family has an American escort, a young man who says to us, "You cannot begin to believe the village life they came from. Southeast Asia. You just could never imagine. Talk about culture shock—they're going to be Californians by morning."

THERE is no time for jet lag or even unpacking when we arrive home. The spirit must be made welcome at once. Rudy builds a wooden pillar for the little temple, facing it to look out our floor-to-ceiling glass windows, into a forest of tall pines. He spends two days in craft shops, finding tiny plastic miniatures that mirror our own belongings—a spotted dog and little white cat, a tray of tropical fruit, a plate of vegetables, and an elephant for transportation—to give honor to the Buddha. In his newly furnished home with a view, the good spirit is settling in.

One night a week later, Rudy and I are asleep in our downstairs bedroom when the phone rings. I am tempted to ignore it, but it rings and rings. When I answer a neighbor is crying, yelling into the phone.

"Get out. Get out. There's a fire in your woods, a fire right behind your house. Hurry."

I rouse Rudy and open our drapes. The fire is tall and crackling in the trees, ringing our home, within feet of our wooden deck. The rest is a blur. I remember corralling our dog and cat to drive down a fire-bordered driveway, returning to beg Rudy to abandon his hose and hopes, at last finding a volunteer fire unit that had time for our home.

Hours later, the fire apparently extinguished, Rudy and I, the German Shepherd Beau Jensen, the little white cat Liza June Jensen, and three firemen rest on couches and carpets while we take turns watching for stray embers. As does the good spirit.

CHAPTER SEVENTEEN

BALI
1991
INDONESIA

THIS IS THE STORY ABOUT HOW WE COME TO VISIT TWO BALIS.

"Are you finding it harder to make plans that please both of you?" the cover of the women's magazine asks. Inside, it poses the follow-up question: "Is compromise a dying art in your marriage?"

If so, the remedy is: "Turn-taking."

Marital harmony from turn-taking. I propose that instead of struggling to agree on an itinerary in Bali, we each design one half of our days on the island. Rudy cannot contain a wide smile. As we know, he is not by nature a planner, but then he rarely gets to envision a trip without some of my, shall we say, assistance. He strips our public library of texts on Indonesian arts while I study slick travel magazines with articles that favorably compare new Balinese resorts to four-star, world-class hotels. We are the ideal couple to test turn-taking theory.

In the 1990s, the Western world knows little about the Shangri-La that is Bali, but major hotel chains export to its shores a few multi-story hotels, harbingers of development to come. From the airport, we enter a gated beachfront compound secreting away the resort I have selected. The hotel is as advertised: isolated, elegant, built of native woods amidst manicured lawns, both Western and Eastern menus in its restaurant. It also offers mounds of luggage in the lobby, a paging system that calls shrilly for tour group members, and rows of weathered tourists wearing, at best, far-too-small bikinis on the private beach. Securely fenced off from Bali residents, the beach has mutual benefit. Tourists want "protection" from locals, and locals want not to view topless sunbathers, an affront to their sense of civility.

Nightly entertainment is on a massive stage in a vast tropical garden. Seated in upholstered lounge chairs, we are served by cocktail waitresses in elaborate native costumes. An announcer with a British accent narrates a short dance story, one Rudy recognizes as loosely based on a traditional Balinese legend.

"This must be some kind of Cliff's Notes production," he whispers.

In the interest of enjoying my turn, I concentrate on

massages, yoga classes, room service breakfast, and happy hours on the beach. Rudy buries himself in his art books. He knows the ground rules of turn-taking and exerts great energy to stifle his disappointment at this too-polished hotel.

It is, though, clearly time for a compromise. I do not admit it aloud, but after a week I am beginning to feel resort life borders on the boring. Perhaps I am over-pummeled by masseuses, overstretched by yoga masters. Frighteningly, I realize there is a chance I am converting to Rudy's Rules for Travel. This marriage may be losing its delicate balance.

He and I agree to spend time at neighboring Sanur, a quiet public beach and small town a few miles away. Each day we walk up the road, past the taxis lined up in front of our resort, and flag down a modest cab, or occasionally one of Rudy's preferred *bemos*. These old vans have seats removed and two long benches installed along the sides so that passengers face each other knee to knee, securing ducks or other food sources between their limbs. Even in the broiling, sticky temperature of the afternoons, there seems no limit to the number of human and livestock passengers that can be stuffed onto the benches. When necessary, assorted arms, legs, and cages hang out either side of the groaning vehicle.

At Sanur we walk the quiet beach, with our same daily routine of following behind the kite man with his huge, brilliantly colored box-shaped kites flying high, meant to reach the gods. Rudy spends hours wondering how a kite might come home with him.

"There has got to be a way . . . I can see it flying from our deck at home."

I am getting ample entertainment just from picturing

him moving down the airliner aisle with his five-foot-square maroon box kite. We are gearing up for one of those flights home when I will agree not to complain about his souvenir if he will agree not to tell anyone I know him.

The Balinese we meet on the beach or in the small town, young and old, ask the same questions in the same order and rhythm. It's clear some kind of Tourist Bureau is augmenting their gracious nature with a little formal English training.

"Allo."

"Why come Bali?"

"How long you be in Bali?"

"You like Bali?"

"Where you stay Bali?"

There is no pause between questions in the drill, no time for us to answer. I can understand, as it is harder for me, too, to receive a foreign language than speak it.

We find a beachfront open-air children's dance school, and an instructor in ceremonial dress gestures for us to take seats on a bench amidst a dozen young—perhaps eight-year-old—boys. Rudy has a terrified look. As a school principal, he knows a lot about eight-year-old boys. But in moments, we see there is a difference. For over an hour, the little buddhas on the bench soundlessly, intently study dance moves of their classmates. Behind us, slightly older children practice over and over the sounds of the flute, gong, and xylophone. As each small group of dancers completes their routine, little ones observing bow their heads toward them in respect. This is not the American playground.

RUDY'S turn. It is time to head to far simpler lodging in the village of Ubud. While I pack for the trip into the hills of Bali, Rudy sets out to find our ride. There is never a shortage of tour buses, passenger vans, and taxis lined up in the driveway of the resort, but still I sense a need to set ground rules:

I make sure I have Rudy's attention, look him in the eye, and say slowly and clearly, "Promise me you won't load me into a *bemo*."

"Not a problem," he says. "No *bemo*."

(Sometimes you have to repeat.) "Promise me you won't load me into a *bemo*. This is a long trip up into the hills, and we have luggage to bring."

He is disappointed. Clearly, he has already struck some deal with the local *bemo* driver.

He sighs and looks down. "I get it. No *bemo*."

An hour or so later, while I am standing at the hotel desk counting out traveler's checks to pay our bill, I hear the first sounds, a combination of wheezing and metallic scraping with occasional screeching. They grow louder. The desk clerk can see the fear in my eyes, if not sense my racing pulse.

He tries to explain. "Dee-livrey. Old truck. Dee-livrey road no."

I understand that he thinks an aged delivery truck has missed the hotel's delivery driveway and is now heading unbidden toward the serene portico, the resort entry. I know it is an aged truck, and I know Rudy is bringing it for me.

He has walked out of the resort and up to the main road, flagged down an ancient one-ton truck with mud-stained, battered wood paneling and flatbed, jumped aboard, and returned to gather our possessions and me.

"Hi, honey!" he waves and shouts out the window, grinning widely, eyes flashing. "We're heeere!"

I approach slowly, attempting to collect a variety of thoughts.

"You think we're riding up the mountain in this, this thing?" I grit my teeth and speak quietly, not wanting to offend the beaming, proud truck owner. "Just exactly where do I sit?"

"Right up front. The driver's bench will do if we all cozy up."

"With the driver?"

"Well, yes. Hadi is a very nice man, a good friend. And I'll sit over the gear box if you want."

My astonishment is nothing compared to that of the resort staff. A small crowd gathers around us—housekeepers, gardeners, and the desk clerk. In unison, they shake their heads and roll sad eyes. I understand little of what they say, but I hear a few English words, like "brakes" and "tires." In a country accustomed to all forms of public vehicles, this truck apparently sets a new low.

Hadi, a short, thin man, perhaps thirty or forty years old, climbs down from the high seat of the truck and with a big smile, extends his hand to me. "Friend," he says, "friend." I have a feeling he has just now learned that word and that this is his first venture as a tour guide. I also have a feeling Rudy is his new business manager.

The ride up the sculptured terraced hills to Ubud is an even mix of physical torture and visual enchantment. Rudy and I lock arms, hoping to compensate for worn-out, stretched-out seat belts, using the weight of our bodies to stay closer to the truck's bench than to its roof. Hadi is in fact a nice man, swerving to avoid the largest of potholes, slowing whenever I scream, and pointing out the most beautiful of rice fields. He is, if anything, too solicitous, turning to console me after each hairpin turn.

I seek Rudy's help. "Can you please ask him to look at the road?"

Hadi does indeed get us safely to Ubud. Rudy has chosen a simple bungalow in the compound of a well-known Dutch painter who moved to Indonesia, converted to Hinduism, married a Balinese woman, and became an Indonesian citizen. I know from the moment we alight from the truck that Rudy has found his role model. We are in the outskirts of the village, next to rice fields and a ravine, here before tourism will discover the hills. The property is simple, serene. Our neighbors also live in compounds, with high walls encircling generations of families, common kitchens and living areas, shrines and gardens. I have to admit I already like this setting even more than the beaches.

After bowing his head before the small shrine on our bungalow porch, Hadi stays to sit with us, drinking a cup of welcome tea served on a rattan tray by a young woman in ceremonial dress. He and Rudy, with a combination of sign language and some sort of pidgin, plan trips to places where, guaranteed, no other tourist will be found. I hesitate to interrupt their reverie, but the survival instinct rules.

"Rude, we aren't going on these trips in that truck, are we?"

"Well, yes. That's Hadi's truck."

"But . . ."

"Turn-taking, remember? Turn-taking."

I quieted. He is, after all, the man who at the resort paid five dollars for a cup of coffee, and who sat with a wide collection of tourists through dance program after dance program without a complaint. I tell myself that I will be more cautious in the future—no more trusting the slick magazines for travel or marital advice.

We settle into a routine, waking at dawn each morning to find trays of cakes and coffee and black rice pudding on our doorstep, along with a fresh offering for our shrine: a thin palm frond interwoven with tropical flowers into a square-shaped, flat bouquet. Rudy has never understood why travelers waste their time in meditation when there is a world to see, but here on the porch he sits each morning and studies the offering, turning it from side to side, holding it to the sunlight. "I need to learn how to make these at home," he says.

On day one, Hadi finds a festival at a small temple high in the hills. Police have closed the road, allowing a spectacular procession of villagers that stretches as far as we can see. With Hadi, we join them, staying at the far edges of the path that will take us to the sacred site. Women of the village, attired in vibrant, gold-threaded ceremonial dress, glide, rather than merely walk, beside us, balancing tall headdresses of carefully stacked layers of fruits and cakes. They look straight ahead, their steps measured, hand motions perfectly keeping time with strains of the gamelan's bamboo and bronze instruments. Reaching the temple gates, the women kneel slowly, carefully removing and leaving on the steps their headdresses, bountiful gourmet offerings to the gods. Even in the midst of tradition and elegance, it is hard to not be a pragmatic American.

"Rude, do you think they bring everything to a food bank after dark?"

"I'm sure the spirits know what to do."

The following days are dedicated to The Search. Once more violating his own rule against large souvenirs, Rudy wants to bring home a Balinese woodcarving. I have been on his searches before. I have hunted for the brightest silver belt buckle in Mexico, the loudest but cheapest cuckoo clock in Germany, the almost-free-of-charge silk robe in a Thai night market. I suspect now that I will see every carving in Mas, the neighboring village where the gods themselves bestow skills upon wood carvers.

I suspect also that this mission will be another training session for Hadi as he launches his newly announced business, "The Real Bali Tours." Rudy has not been able to leave his teacher role at home; he and Hadi meet on the porch early each morning to practice English and design a colorful sign for the battered truck. Today, I find our trainer standing face to face with our driver, some ten feet apart, holding a pair of scissors in one hand, gesturing toward the space between them.

"He needs to learn about the middleman, hon."

"Okay. And the scissors are for what?"

"Simple—(cut, cut)—we are cutting out the middleman. This is a demonstration."

It is becoming clear that the search for the perfect wood carving will not take place in comfortable, air-cooled art galleries of Mas, the ones pictured in tourist brochures. I change from sandals to ugly but sturdy walking shoes, for we are cutting out the middleman.

After a quick reconnaissance of sample galleries in Mas, studying especially their asking prices, Rudy directs Hadi down the back roads of the village. Yesterday's rains have muddied our path, but the truck lumbers on until Rudy spots a back alley with stacks of tree roots and branches, raw materials for elegant Balinese art. We leave our truck in a clearing and begin to walk, peeking into windows and open doors, looking for artists who supply works to the galleries. Rudy moves past the carvers who are making what look like identical statues of a Balinese dancer.

"That's just what happens," he says, "a few Americans come along and buy the same carving and word spreads. Every carver for fifty miles copies it, over and over. We need to get off the beaten path to get something unique."

I could have sworn we had left the beaten path long before. We are an oddity in the back passages—adults, children, even the dogs look at us with a mix of suspicion and puzzlement.

On day two of The Search, we spot a small alcove along the side of an alley, where three carvers, probably of three generations, work on what Hadi says is a large, single hibiscus root. Their knives shear off only thin layers of the root; at this pace they must not produce more than one sculpture a month. We see in the corner of the small yard only one finished piece, a four-foot bird carved from root. I remember that Michelangelo is said to have insisted he had not carved David of marble; rather, David had emerged from marble. Here, an elegant soaring bird, wings spread wide, head thrust back and mouth open, long, narrow legs balanced on the root base, flies from the hibiscus.

The piece is beautiful, creative, unique, but oh so delicate.

"**AND** how will this get home?" I ask.

Anticipating my question, a woman and two young children emerge from a doorway, dragging a large box, big enough for a chest of drawers or an oven. The carving will take perhaps one fourth of the carton space, and in gestures they demonstrate that the bird will be wrapped and wrapped until he is snug in the large cocoon. To illustrate, the woman uses strips of rag to wrap one wing securely. Rudy is sold.

Preparation of the bird for his first flight takes hours. The family is proud of its work, Hadi translates, and wants it to travel safely to America, California. They turn three barrels upside down and gesture for Rudy, Hadi, and me to sit. The children bring tea in battered cups, then sit cross-legged on the ground close to us.

This is one of those times I wish I could be more like my spouse. He is mesmerized, sipping his tea and intently studying the carvers at work. I am trying to recall all I have read about cholera and teacups.

LATE that night, we are squeezed into Hadi's front seat heading toward tonight's regional *kecak*, or monkey, dance. In rainy daylight, unpaved roads between small, remote hill towns challenge drivers with muddy potholes, collapsing shoulders, and roaming dogs. Night multiplies the threat. As the rain and darkness increase, Hadi spots friends by the roadside waiting for a *bemo*. He is visibly upset, as he and the Americans ride in such great comfort while his friends stand in the dark in a growing storm.

"We need to pick up those poor souls, don't you think?" Rudy says. "But where do we put them?"

Hadi rescues seven or eight men and women and shelters them under tarps in the back of the truck. The trip is slower now as the vintage vehicle adjusts to its new load, and by the time we reach the makeshift dance site, a dirt floor with portable metal roofing, most benches are filled. Our passengers approach Rudy and me, bowing slightly and gesturing to a bench in the midst of the crowd where the Balinese audience has squeezed together to make room for us all. We will sit there and I will fight back tears. I am, after all, the one who thought the truck so unsuitable.

The performers, perhaps one hundred men robed in cloths hung round their waists, sit in concentric circles on the ground before us. There is no orchestra. For over an hour, the men are their own percussion, bouncing, swaying, moving arms and hands faster and faster, sweating, chanting like the monkey, "cak-a, chark-a," until a fevered pitch is reached and our benches seem to sway. Someone lights a bonfire in the center of the circles and the chant becomes hypnotic. Performers near us are in what look like trance states, and they seem to be taking us with them.

After some time, the fire and the rhythm of the monkeys very, very gradually slow down until the flame is extinguished and the performers sit resting. As the intensity of the night decreases, we all sit back, watching colorfully clad dancers enter the circle and through music and motion tell the tale of two young princes, a demon king, a damsel in distress, and a mischievous monkey.

We leave our passengers in front of their small family compound, a long way from the street where we first met. As we drive toward our bungalow, Rudy puts his arm around me and talks quietly. "I was really proud of you tonight. I know how deathly afraid of fire you are, and we were packed into the middle of that crowd, but you never said a word."

"Fire? That's right . . . I remember fire, but I don't remember fear."

True, it was not the performers alone who were in altered states this night.

RUDOLF S. JENSEN
33738257
Class 44-16

Chapter Eighteen

TIBENHAM
1992
ENGLAND

RUDY PULLS UP A CHAIR OPPOSITE MINE AT OUR BREAKFAST table and looks at me intently in that way that says he has a lot on his mind.

"I think it's time. I want to go there . . . no, it's not that I really want to. I guess it's that I need to."

The "there" I know is Tibenham, an English village of

less than five hundred residents, where very little happens now. Over fifty years ago, a lot was happening. Tibenham housed a major airbase from which the American Eighth Air Force launched attacks on Nazi Germany. Success came at a price: the division suffered one of the highest casualty rates of American air forces in World War II, many occurring in a single mission.

I have two pictures of Rudy from that time. In the first, a handsome, healthy, smiling young recruit in dress uniform looks into the camera and the world with confidence. In the second, a far older, thinner airman with pursed lips stares straight ahead through dark eyes, eyes that must have seen too much. Four months of training as a B-24 gunner separate the photos.

The first is a portrait of a man I know well, the man I travel with. I meet the second man only occasionally, never in travel but late at night at home, when he tosses bedding and mutters about being late or writing his parents or being shot from the sky.

Rudy has not forgotten or even willed to forget World War II. He is a student of military history, reading account after account of strategy and combat. He has visited Churchill's War Rooms, Hitler's Eagle Nest. He has pored over the Imperial War and Eighth Air Force museum collections, and he has walked D-Day beaches and knelt at American cemeteries in Europe, those unbearably sad places with their rows and rows of white crosses. At each resting place, Rudy has looked for names on the crosses, names that might be familiar, noted the ages of twenty-year-olds, twenty-five-year-olds.

But Tibenham, his own airbase, is different. In fact, we have come very near the town several times in our travels. We have been on British trains that stopped at Norwich station, twenty kilometers from the village, but we have never gotten off. "Someday I'll want to see it again," he would say. "I'm just not sure when."

On this rainy, gray winter day, nearly fifty years from his service there, Rudy and I are on a train approaching Norwich station. He has written ahead to a memorial center, asking to see his old base. Subdued, he takes down our overnight cases, and without a word, he descends the train steps. A middle-aged man on the platform spots us immediately, apparently from the photo Rudy has sent.

"Sergeant Jensen, Yes? Rudolf? I am Neal. Welcome back, sir. Welcome, Mrs. Jensen."

He offers firm handshakes and what I take to be an encouraging smile. "We have some people waiting to see you here in Norwich. We'd like to start your homecoming here before you visit Tibenham tomorrow, if that suits you."

Rudy is visibly relieved that this return can be done in stages.

Neal's station wagon takes us downtown to a large, modern public library where a librarian greets us on the doorstep. Following her through a colorful children's area and a dignified history section, we come to the 2nd Air Division U.S. Memorial Library, a spacious, comfortable reading and research area with shelves of World War II tomes, films, photographs, personal diaries, and papers, all documenting sacrifices American airmen made here. Next to the war documents is a lending library of all things Americana, past and present: our histories, cookbooks, travel guides, magazines, and novels. Many of my favorite books are on these shelves. Being in their company soothes me.

Rudy recalls that, as the war came to an end and the American airbase began to close, airmen donated funds to leave a memorial behind.

"One of the officers said an endowed library could tell future generations the story of what happened here. My friends and I were just kids—we didn't know what an endowment was, but we emptied our savings accounts and left a lot behind. We loved the Brits. They were so kind to us."

Neal has an interpretation. "I think they treated you as heroes and you rose to the occasion, no matter how young you were. You'll meet Matthew soon. He has never forgotten you were saviors."

As if on cue, a graying gentleman, perhaps in his sixties, dressed in tweed suit and a tie, studies the library calendar where Rudy's name is listed as today's guest. He turns to us.

"Are you really Mr. Jensen? I'm Matthew. I probably know you."

And with that introduction, Matthew becomes our escort protector. He refuses to eat dinner with us, saying, "That would not be right." Instead, he waits at the door of the restaurant until we walk out, then shadows us to our bed and breakfast and gives a slight wave good night. "I be sure you're safe."

The next morning our innkeeper Elizabeth knocks on our door before breakfast. "Matthew is here," she says. "He wants to sit at the table next to you and be with you while you eat. He won't allow you to buy him breakfast, but he'll take a cup of tea from me. He just wants to be near you."

Rudy is puzzled. "He said he may know me . . ."

"He may," she says. "You remember when you were here, food was scarce for villagers—there was at times such hunger, such trauma." Elizabeth turns to me to explain. "In the afternoons, American airmen would share their ration kits, handing them through the wire fence to children waiting there. Matthew was one of those children. At holidays they'd give a party for the little ones—so many sweets! Matthew remembers it all."

"I do too," Rudy tells us. "I remember the children and the fence."

We eat breakfast in silence. Matthew, dressed again in suit and tie, seems more comfortable not talking, and Rudy is engrossed in his own thoughts. Every few bites, we three make a little eye contact and offer shy smiles. As we finish, Neal appears and is ready to be our guide to Tibenham base. Matthew waves good-bye, but Rudy and I cannot leave him behind. He is too much a part of the story. He starts to say "It would not be right," but Neal puts his arm around him and the two of them show us to the car.

"There are some changes at the base, Rudy," Neal begins as we head onto the road. "Your barracks are gone but a few huts are still there. The new Gliding Club uses one of them as canteen and office. The old control tower is gone, but it was haunted anyway by that airman ghost who wandered its rooms all night."

Rudy nods. He has heard many stories about the ghost and believes some of them. "What about the tall spire on All Saints Church? When we flew in after a mission and spotted that spire, we knew we had survived one more time. Made believers of us all."

"The church spire is there, waiting for you. And so are the members of the Gliding Club. Want to go for a ride and see it again?"

I am glad to be on the ground visiting with two war brides, village women who met and married U.S. airmen, and their husbands, both mechanics here during the war. Matthew declines a ride too, instead sitting alertly behind me until Rudy and Neal make their return glider run. When they do, Matthew opens the door for me and we go outside to see them flying past the church tower and onto the runway. Rudy is thrilled with his ride, even though getting out of the glider is harder than getting in. We all sit at a weathered wooden round table in the canteen, having tea, talking of today's flight. Before long, Neal turns to Rudy.

"You must get tired of talking about this, but I saw in the directory that you were born in Germany, that you became a U.S. citizen in the armed forces."

"Right," Rudy says. "I always thought they must have been running out of airmen to have accepted a German Enemy Alien, and then let him volunteer to fly over Germany— and the son of a Hitler loyalist no less."

Neal is startled at this last detail, but he has more questions.

"I'm probably like everybody else, wondering what let you war against your land of birth. Do you ever share that?"

"Well, it's not very complicated. Papa was loyal to Hitler but I thought of myself as an American. I was so angry at the German government. They brought horror to my homeland. I just wanted to help stop them. I never looked back."

"And your parents? What did they say?"

"They didn't talk at all, not about my going to war or about our relatives still in Germany. On the morning I left, Papa gave me a long and strong hug and said, 'Good luck to you in whatever lies ahead.' That was a lot coming from that man. There was such a terrible tension between us once the war started."

"Well, then, you left one set of tensions for another set, Rudy. You were here at the base during the Kassel Mission, weren't you?"

"Yes, yes I was," Rudy answers, his voice uncommonly soft. "Actually, I was supposed to fly that night. Our crew was all suited up, briefed and ready to go, but at the very last minute the commanding officer took us off the flight list. He said we were too new and hadn't finished enough night orientation training. We put up a fight, but in the end another crew flew to Kassel in our place. We were so angry at the time. We had to fly thirty-five missions before we could go back home. We complained to anyone who seemed to be listening. How would we ever finish thirty-five if they denied us chances to fly?"

"That night," Neal explains, "thirty-seven planes left base. Kassel was a German rail and industrial center, such an important target if the war was to be ended. They were manufacturing aircraft and tanks there. They had to be stopped."

Rudy nods. "Several of the crews were from my barracks. The next afternoon, they were due back at 1:40, so after lunch, a friend and I rode bikes out to the control tower to welcome home our buddies. I noticed a lot of officers standing at the upper rails looking through binoculars. I should have known then, but it was strange—I couldn't let myself think. We stood there waiting, watching the sky for the longest time. Finally, two of our B-24s came straight in with wheels down, shooting off red flares."

Neal says, "Red flares mean wounded men aboard, don't they?"

Rudy bites his lip. His voice breaks but he insists on telling the story.

"Right. Ambulances roared in and we waited for the rest of the planes. After hours, three more came in, and they were so damaged—riddled with holes—we didn't know how they could have stayed in the air. My friend and I couldn't make ourselves leave. The officers told us there would be no more planes, that we should go, but we kept scanning the skies over and over anyway. Thirty-two of our planes and our crews were missing, lost."

Neal puts his hand on Rudy's shoulder as he tells the rest of us, "It was the greatest loss to a single group in aviation history. Rudy, it must have been so hard for you and your crew to fly out of this base after that."

While he takes time to answer, the rest of us put our heads down, look at the table. Rudy reaches for my hand. "It was really hard. Especially at first. After dinner that night, we walked back to our barracks and saw just empty bunks. It was terrible. Their bedding and belongings—all traces of those men—they were gone, as if they had never been there. It was the same in the newspapers, here and back home. No one wanted to talk about those planes and those men. They said it was bad for morale."

"Sometimes it's hard to be left behind too," Neal says.

I think of the tangled bedding in our bedroom at home.

Rudy rubs his eyes. "It is hard to be left behind. My crew still had our thirty-five missions to go, and we understood the risks now. The next day, those of us left in our barracks sat in a circle. We made a lot of promises to each other . . . we would never again take life for granted, we'd make every day count. And we sure as hell would never again fight to be put on a mission list."

He flashes a bit of a rueful smile, then stands and opens the door. "I just need a few minutes. I'll be back soon."

I stand too. My impulse is to follow him, but Neal puts his hand lightly on my arm. "Think about it—usually it's better if the men struggle with their own ghosts," he says. "When he returns, I have a place to take him where we can all go."

I move to the largest window, watching the figure, slightly bent over, walk slowly to the runway. How different this is from our other trips. In other places we go sightseeing together; here Rudy goes soul-searching alone. I can only watch him try.

One of the veterans who had been a mechanic here stands behind me, puts his hand on my shoulder. "It was always so hard to see those young guys go up in that sky. This is pretty hard too."

A half hour or so goes by before Rudy returns. He seems sturdier, but no less sad. Neal drives us to the rectory of the parish church where we meet the sacristan. He knows Rudy has come to visit the spire, but first he brings us into the church, showing us carefully stitched covers on each kneeling bench, and a bank of lighted votive candles.

"The embroidery pieces are from American families of your troops, sent to thank the village for taking care of their young sons. The candles are lighted even now by villagers, thanking you for what you did here."

WE have brought with us a set of letters to share with Neal, perhaps copy for the library. In each one, Rudy writes Mutti, his German stepmother, and Papa, the Hitler loyalist, telling them what he can about his life, trying to reassure them, but, following censorship rules, not revealing his location or missions. Each is handwritten on lined paper torn from a notebook. One is dated 24 December 1944, from England, three months after the Kassel Mission.

Dear Mom and Dad,

Just a few lines to let you all know I'm thinking of you and to tell you all that I am alright.

I guess I couldn't let tonight go without writing you, for as you can see it is Christmas Eve. It's just about 9:30 and after I finish writing this, I'm going to get dressed and get ready for the Midnight Mass. Out of all the times in the year, I'm sure this is the one when I miss home the most. For some reason, all afternoon I've been looking at my watch and matching the time against what I would be doing if I were home. All those memories of our past Christmases together keep coming back to me, and I just can't seem to realize that we are 3,000 miles apart.

To many families in their homes here in England I suppose Christmas is very real. The night is cold and clear. The air is crisp and clean, and there are a million stars flashing and glittering up in the deep blue. The moon is in its first quarter, and someone with an imagination as vivid as mine could easily assume that its silvery light shed over this English countryside is a thin blanket of snow.

Even though it's the same barracks, the same guys, and our same Army clothes, there still is the feeling that tonight is very different. No carols, no tree, no surprise packages, no soft lights or pungent smells of candles and pine needles here. But it's still Christmas Eve and I guess it always will be for me no matter where I am.

I hope I haven't bored you with my thoughts tonight, but it feels so much better to put in writing what has been turning over in my head all day. So I'll leave you for now, with the sincere wish that you both have a happy Christmas together. Let's hope that next year we'll be able to resume our Christmas of old. Till the next time, then, good night.

Your Son, Rudy

He is twenty-three years old this night. I am two months old, celebrating my first Christmas. At my house there is a tree, surprise packages, soft lights, carols.

CHAPTER NINETEEN

THE OLD RADIO HAS MORE CRACKLE THAN CONTENT, BUT IT is the only link between today's fiftieth anniversary celebrations and our small Provence kitchen this night of June 6, D-Day. I have my French-to-English dictionary ready, but the words from the radio flow within a storm of emotion, tears, cries as French men and women, older than I but not by much, tell of that night and of that day in 1944.

We know the numbers. One hundred sixty thousand Allied troops came across the sea that night; ten thousand lost lives or independence. Today the older Allied veterans of the battles invade France once again—some in parachutes, most in tour buses—to honor their fallen comrades. In Avignon this morning, I stopped at a newspaper stand to buy commemorative editions for Rudy, whole newspapers with photos and full-page banner headlines. "Men of War Celebrate Peace in Their Time," one says. "*Merci beaucoup*, Allies," another shouts.

On the radio tonight, one woman speaks in a mix of French and English. I silently thank my high school French teacher, for I can understand a bit. "I was child, child sitting on a hillside, watching boats come in. I was afraid they come to hurt me. My mother said, 'No, no, these are friends. They come to save.' I know now. They friends, come to save me."

In other interviews, the phrases repeat: "*Merci, merci*," they say one by one, "*Merci pour* lives, *merci pour liberté*."

I translate what I can for Rudy, for nearly an hour. "The French are so grateful."

"I guess I needed to be with them, to hear that," he says.

"I don't understand. Of course they're grateful."

"Well, it's not as simple as that. In war you meet death so many times. You bring death. You have to keep convincing yourself that you're really bringing life. I liked hearing about the little girl."

Chapter Twenty

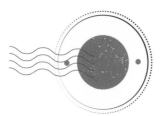

Cruises: Dipping Down into the Bucket

OVER TIME, AND IN A SLOW PROCESS, MULTIPLE FORCES conspire to erode the enforcement of Rudy's Rules. The first is unplanned exposure to cruise ships.

We arrive in Seattle on a summer day, poised to board the

Alaskan ferry for a weeklong journey with my mother and niece, Cindy. I call to confirm our reservations.

"You must have missed the news," the operator says. "The ferry workers have been on strike all week."

I begin my lamentations promptly and loudly.

"Ma'am, ma'am," she tries to interrupt. "Take a deep breath. You know, 1 . . . 2 . . ."

How does she know about that?

"The cruise ship, The Sun Princess, is accepting your party."

All of us except Rudy are jubilant at the approximately one thousand percent free upgrade.

"I can't believe this is happening to me," he says. "You know how much I want to ride the ferry."

I do know. I have watched him pack for the ferry like a Boy Scout, adding a canteen, small bedroll, and down jacket to his wardrobe of faded jeans and plaid shirts. He has read that in order to have the true Alaskan experience, one must sleep on deck under the starry skies.

I respond sympathetically. "We need to get to a mall fast and find a Nordstrom. We each have to have at least one good outfit. There'll be a captain's dinner and—"

"We need to take two cars."

Rudy has a shopping destination he will not reveal, and I suspect his cruise attire will be found at K-Mart. I am wrong. The local thrift store has a rack of six-dollar navy blazers, and if you roll up the sleeves and pin them just right, no one is the wiser. A limp almost-white shirt and one red tie complete the outfit.

"This is the last cruise I'm ever going on," he explains, "so

I can't invest in clothes. Cruises are so artificial—people spend two hours in a Mexican tourist trap and claim they've seen the country."

This opinion is rendered before he boards the cruise liner and finds the seafood buffet, the midnight chocolate spread, and a husband for Cindy.

✈

JOHN, the handsome British deck steward, sees us on deck, all lined up in our chaise lounges, wrapped in warm blankets and ready to sail. He notices Cindy first, of course, then Rudy who is reading Cornelius Ryan's *The Last Battle*. A conversation starter. After their joint analysis of Ryan's works and much of naval history, Rudy gets to the point.

"Have you met our niece?"

And to Cindy, once the young man reluctantly leaves us to attend to customers: "That nice man really likes you. You should find him and talk to him."

Anyone who is a student of Cornelius Ryan would clearly make a perfect life companion.

My mother has the gift (or curse?) of prophecy. Before this day ends she is asking herself, and us, just how she will explain to Cindy's father that the girl has run away to sea.

Beginning the next year, after the wedding, Rudy finds that cruises can occasionally help him reach down into the bucket where the list resides. He never succumbs to those floating cities called megaships, but rather selects barges that float leisurely down the Ohio and Mississippi, crafts that squeeze through the Erie or Panama Canals, or mid-sized ships that sail among glaciers or islands or fjords.

✈

THESE new compromises of the Rules are suiting me well. Perhaps I was born to float in luxury. I have come a long way since the goat on the Luxor ferry ate my sandal, and the barge crew in Mexico fished me from the sea. Standing today on the deck of the small ocean liner, leaning over a rail, I relax and study Tahitian turquoise waters, enjoy the peacefulness of a cruise ship securely docked and without any people. The other passengers, including Rudy, have left for Bora Bora day trips. Some struggle to master diving gear, others snorkel, still others like Rudy circle overhead in small, perilous helicopters. I have chosen standing on the top deck as the safest of options.

"No," I told Rudy earlier this morning. "I'm not going on a helicopter trip. I haven't forgotten the Kauai copter."

"Kauai copter" is code for "all-time most terrifying travel experience I will not repeat." Nearly ten years ago on that island, Rudy persuaded me to take my first helicopter ride over admittedly lush landscape.

"It's the only way we'll be able to see the Na Pali coast," he had said then. "It's a natural treasure. You can't miss it."

I need to tell you that in order to see that beauty, you must open your eyes. That is something I could not do that day. The middle-aged copter shuddered as it rose hesitantly from its pad. Seated behind the young, casually attired pilot, I realized he did not keep eyes on the cliffs looming ahead nor hands on the controls. The copter bobbed about while he talked and laughed with co-pilot Rudy and the male passenger beside me. The three were having fun. I was not.

A few minutes after liftoff, my complex moral dilemma arose. I had been accustomed to managing fear, or even terror, but this situation had an added dimension of social responsibility. Just behind my left ear a soft rattling noise grew louder and louder until it came to a high pitch, sounding much like a large bolt being shaken in a glass jar. A very fragile glass jar. As we flew on, the pilot never turned to check for the source of the sound. The copter just kept bobbing, getting closer and closer to the steep cliffs of Na Pali. I spent the flight, eyes closed and deep breathing in progress, pondering my responsibility to the pilot, to Rudy, to the other passenger. Should I warn them that an essential part was loose, that we were about to plunge into the sea? Perhaps he and the passenger had young children.

An element of social sensitivity was also involved. If we were to survive after my call to alarm, it would be embarrassing. I had a lot to weigh in my decision, finally concluding that it was better to feign bravery and spare any insult to my pride. After all, my knowledge of helicopter parts was rather limited.

I lived through the Kauai copter experience. When we landed, neither the pilot nor I spoke of the bolt. But now here in Bora Bora is Rudy, rushing across the ship's deck toward me, calling my name, interrupting my reverie.

"Aren't you back early?" I ask, struggling to keep disappointment out of my voice. I had so looked forward to peace and stillness. "I thought your flight was at least an hour."

"Oh, Mare, I had to cut it short so I could come get you.

You have got to see this place from the air. It is the most beautiful lagoon in the world. You can't miss it. Forget Kauai. This will be so different. It's a new helicopter and the pilot is mature, seems to be some kind of navy captain."

This has my attention. I have to admit I have heard the islets surrounding Bora Bora are extraordinary, and from the ship they look only like pale pancakes spread on water. And besides, I am touched that my spouse would cut his own trip short to come get me, and that he would find a navy captain to carry us safely.

It is true. The helicopter is new and the pilot is a middle-aged man attired in a navy military jacket with multiple stripes and medals, surely signifying bravery and competence. He stands at attention beside the copter door, then helps me into the backseat, salutes me.

"See, hon, I told you this would be a safe ride," Rudy says proudly.

As advertised, we fly gently with seabirds over the bluest of blue lagoons, shades of the color shifting, mixing below us. Rudy grins, points out one heart-shaped islet.

One hour later, we land with soft precision on an open beachfront strip.

"This will be another picture for your Victory Shelf," Rudy says, readying his camera. We started my Victory Shelf at home to display my moments of untoward bravery, times I have conquered fear and mistrust. The shelf is a little bare so far, displaying three photos, one showing the day I was five and sat upon a pony, another celebrating my climb all the way to the top of Saint Peter's roof, the third picturing me afloat in a zodiac amidst Alaskan glaciers. This would be photo number four. Full disclosure: Once you set foot in St. Peter's staircase, there is no turning back—it is one way, so despite your cries, you climb. As for Alaskan zodiacs, they are far less threatening if you wear two life vests and drink one glass of wine.

Rudy takes my picture as I smile, give a thumbs up, show no worry creases.

I climb out of the backseat of the helicopter just in time to see our captain take off the navy jacket with the shiny medals and return it to a man waiting for him on the beach.

✈

RUDY sees an ad for a British ocean liner, one combining renowned lecturers with English high teas and unique itineraries. "Papa talked about sailing to Spitzbergen," Rudy says, "and I'd love to spend time with the Brits. We need to take this trip."

What I need to do is read itineraries more carefully. If I had, I would not now be surprised that the ship travels on open seas for two days, sailing far past the tip of Norway, above the Arctic Circle. I blame the trip brochure; it shows the journey in three inches, picturing the far northern destination just around the corner from Tromsø. Every few hours, I visit the gleaming blue globe in the ship's library, trying to ascertain just when we will find the destination sitting at the top of the sphere. In his daily briefing over the ship's microphone, our captain announces that we are traveling in and out of satellite transmission, so there will be no emails, faxes, or phone calls, and a "somewhat altered" ship's navigation system. "This is quite a unique voyage," the captain says. "I find it very interesting. I've never been this far north myself."

Consumer confidence takes a dive except in our cabin. "Wow—he's never been here," says Rudy. "That makes it so much more fun."

The cruise is advertised as "The Journey of the Arctic Tern" in honor of Spitzbergen's summertime residents—slender white birds with dark heads and markings, seasoned travelers that fly 25,000 miles each year to winter at the tip of Antarctica. The crew warn us against wearing anything white ashore, lest the feisty birds mistake us for enemies. "You don't want those little birds to think you're a fox or polar bear," they say. "You don't want them pecking holes in your head."

We agree that if we had to fly 25,000 miles every year, we'd be a little touchy too.

Passengers are told not to approach the tern nesting areas, for the birds are also known to have strong maternal instincts. Besides their skills of aerial bombing, they are especially talented at defending their newborns by camouflage. Rudy and I watch quietly while a tern works to distract us from what appears to be her nest by first dancing around us, then posing for photos right at our feet. We are charmed and flattered at the time, but when we get home, we see that the tern's renowned camouflage leaves us with no decipherable bird image in the developed photo. Clever.

But not even clever terns can distract Rudy from wartime memories that accompany this British ship now sailing back toward Dover. I still want to believe that World War II is long past—it is, after all, the year 2005. But most of our fellow passengers are Rudy's age. The battles may have ended sixty years ago, but the war is today for the British we meet.

Rudy's affection and respect for the English runs deep. I see it in his focused blue eyes, in the way he leans forward during each conversation to catch their every word. Rudy saw the life they lived then—the bombings, rubble, shelters, rationing, and London children transported to farmlands. The British passengers in turn want to know what it was like for the young American assigned to England, and then to the skies filled with enemy fire. I see that in a short time they understand far more about Rudy in those years than I ever will.

As the ship comes to the end of its journey and enters the Dover harbor, Rudy, his camera strung about his neck, finds me. "Come meet me up on the top deck," he says. "Bring two glasses of good red wine, OK?"

I find him on the top forward deck, leaning far over, photographing the chalky, statuesque White Cliffs of Dover, quietly singing the lyrics. "There'll be love and laughter, and peace ever after . . ."

He puts his arm around me, drawing me close. "Whoever wrote that song had no idea just how lovely those cliffs could be."

"You must have flown over them on the way back to Tibenham."

"We did. We'd escape enemy gunfire, fly toward England, finally see the Cliffs rising up ahead of us, then watch them slip under the wings of our plane."

He pauses, takes another photograph. "There were times when our plane was so torn up we didn't know if we would reach them even to say good-bye."

He lifts his glass of wine in a toast toward the White

Cliffs. "Those times we limped in, you were especially beautiful."

AS we experiment with cruising, Rudy has one major criticism of the trips, a wrong he is determined to right. Shore excursions cost too much. He organizes small cost-sharing tours for a few select passengers, but these in general do not go well.

On a small island in Tahiti, he meets a local resident whose van will take us to Major Event, an important day for the island, a festival of some sort, one not mentioned in the ship's calendar. Rudy fills the eight seats of the van and we head off for a bumpy but very short ride to the next village. With fanfare, our driver/guide parks along the side of the road, opens a weathered shed, and pulls out a worn white plastic chair for each person, arranging us in a precise half-circle facing a tall palm tree. We are, he tells us, lucky to be here today, because *today* is the day. Today the island gets its first satellite dish put up on the tree, and we have the best seats.

I personally like the Satellite Event in Tahiti better than the Bird Street Event in Hong Kong. Three unsuspecting fellow cruisers, a young couple and their five-year-old Davey, come with us to tour the vibrant city. Beyond the frenetic pace, the bright lights, the cell phones everywhere, Hong Kong is a world built for Rudy. It has thirteen-cent tram and ferry rides, free public markets, and the colorful Bird Garden.

Parrots, parakeets, canaries, a mynah—birds of brilliant colors hang in elaborately carved cages amongst the trees, chirping, singing, waiting for their mostly elderly owners to finish chess games or conversations. While they wait, the birds mangle and eat their breakfast, a live cricket whose struggle for life captivates Davey and Rudy.

Eventually, the elderly bird owners stop chess and visiting, place cages atop tall bamboo poles, and walk in a bit of a line down the narrow alleys, past the shops selling cages and seed for pampered pets. We follow.

"Where are we going?" I whisper to Rudy.

"It'll be great," he responds. This means he does not know. He is only following the bird cages.

The procession ends at a darkened tea room and our fellow cruisers are reluctant to enter. Rudy, who does not know Chinese, translates the signs on the windows: "Good, cheap tea," "Tourists welcome." A waiter dressed in a colorful, traditional jacket comes to the door to gesture us inside and we all follow. (Maybe the sign does say "Welcome.") We sit at a long table in the center of the tea room, the only table lacking a tall stand for a bird cage. The old men are each sitting in a booth now, directly below their birds hung high along the wall. Our table is covered with previously white, now tea-stained, paper and used teacups left over from the last occupants. No one makes an attempt to clear it and replace the paper.

"Not to worry," Rudy assures us. "Things are very hygienic. Look at how long these people live."

Just as I spot a nest of huge live grasshoppers in the booth to our right, our waiter pushes a cart with a basin of muddy gray water to our table. One by one he lifts each used cup, shakes it in the bath and waves it in the air to dry. Hot brewed tea follows, but our thirst that came on so quickly has now left just as rapidly. We each suddenly remember somewhere we need to be, some commitment in Hong Kong we had forgotten. My commitment is to my hotel room. Rudy is disappointed that his tour is ending early, but he has an idea.

"I'm going to ride the ferries back and forth, learn what the people think about the island returning to China. Got to find out."

He returns to our hotel room hours later. "I found university students who wanted to talk," he says. "It's not a scientific survey, but I would say there are a lot of worried people."

ANOTHER cruise ship docks at a Hawaiian island Rudy knows well. It has a mix of upscale hotels and restaurants, as well as locals' destinations. We know which Rudy prefers. "We're on our way to *authéntico*," he tells two passengers. "This place has cooked the cheapest Hawaiian breakfast for decades—eggs, waffles, Portuguese sausage, free coffee."

The two passengers follow us to the restaurant, looking uneasy as we enter the aged, deserted café and take our seats on worn, wobbly benches. We are the only diners. I am seated beside Rudy and across from Joy and Mark. From where I sit, I have, throughout the bountiful meal, full view of *authéntico* mice running directly behind the couple, chasing each other, darting in and out of holes at the baseboard. I find it hard to converse, even harder to eat what I have to admit looks like a tasty breakfast. I don't know which is the greater distraction, studying the mice in full view or wondering what might be frolicking behind me.

✈

As time goes on, cruise ships and their seductive ways continue to erode implementation of the Rules. Rudy grows older; I grow older too, but not so much. He keeps the cabin drapes closed at night more often now, sleeps in and orders room service breakfast, photographs fjords from a lounge chair on the deck, reads Mark Twain's *Life on the Mississippi* atop the river barge. He still, however, shops for his trips at a well-stocked local thrift store.

And he works to convert younger cruise passengers to the Rules, urging them to abandon the lure of leisurely voyages and embrace the edicts while they can. He usually singles out for his counseling those who sit on the top deck, regardless of weather, watching a foreign port come into sight, reading a book, preferably a history book. ("They have potential," he tells me.) A common starter to the conversation is the bucket list. Most people have not realized the bucket list must be put in chronological order. He corrects the misunderstanding.

"So, where are you traveling next?" he asks. "Hawaii? Well, Hawaii is a beautiful state, but it's a good example of a place you can visit right up to your deathbed. Easy walking, English-speaking, elevators everywhere. Handrails on banisters. Pleasant climate. No, no, the Hawaiian islands can wait. I'd suggest you move Hawaii, cruise liners, and U.S. travel down deeper into the bucket. Have you thought about Thai beaches or Yucatan ruins for now?"

Unbidden, he continues. "You may wonder about going to politically unstable places. Well, there are two ways of looking at them: one, they are dangerous now. Two, they may be more dangerous later."

"In short," he confides, "you have to remember that you'll never be younger. And you'll probably never be healthier. You've just got to grab that brass ring when it comes by. Which reminds me, there's a wonderful carousel in Avignon . . . and have you seen the one that townspeople crafted in Missoula?"

CHAPTER TWENTY-ONE

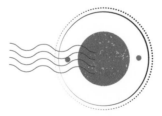

AND OTHER TRANSITIONS

I MAKE THE MISTAKE OF ATTENDING A CONFERENCE OUT of town, leaving Rudy to entertain himself for a week. Home alone. As we have seen, a week is a long time in this man's life.

"I found it," he yells into the phone.

"You found what?"

"Well, it's on approval. If you don't like it, back it goes."

"You found what?"

"Our new RV—actually a fifth-wheeler—twenty-two feet, portable, perfect. You cannot believe the deal we got. I told the salesman you would rule out a used trailer, that we had to get a new one. That was right, wasn't it?"

"It certainly was."

I did not know we were seriously looking for an RV. We have seen a few of these cozy quarters and said that "someday" we would slow down, abandon long, crowded flights in favor of long, leisurely road trips. But as I walk out of the Sacramento airport, I see a bright red and gray Ford truck towing a fifth-wheeler and parked at the "no parking" curb. Rudy hugs me, takes my suitcase, and tosses it into our new home on wheels. While the parking patrolman appears to be waiting patiently, my RV mate escorts me up the steps and points out highlights.

"Look, I have little sheets for the little bed, two towels, a bar of soap, a coffee pot, coffee, two bottles of wine and—" Opening the dorm-size refrigerator, he adds, "Some of that Brie you like, straight from Paris. We're all set, booked for our shakedown trip tonight at an RV park right down the road. You cannot believe the deal I got off-season on that."

I remember the bucket-list rules and know we are taking a significant step tonight. We often say that when foreign travel means physically challenging travel, it is time to see the USA. America has handrails, toilets you can sit on and also rise from, 24-hour food and medical help, grand national parks, and RV campgrounds that look like Westin resorts.

(Note: We won't be staying in those.) In America, we won't wonder how to convert currency, how to balance our days around siesta time. (Well, maybe the siesta tradition can stay.)

For all its contrasts, we learn that first night some commonalities of domestic travel with foreign ventures, namely that the road has challenges but kind strangers appear. On shakedown night, four seasoned RV campers help us back the rig into a tiny space at dark, plug in electricity and sewer lines, and make a bed while lying across it.

So his intention, at least as he describes it, is to become an RV retiree. But I think I detect the old pace hanging on, and I am betting to myself that we will not end our RV phase until we see fifty states. Or rather, until we have seen the states and Canada. He buys a thick, used volume of Canadian history and I know that our itinerary is expanded.

"Rude," I ask at one Montana campground, "how about we sleep in late tomorrow and stay another night here in the mountains?" (That is translation for "Let's not drive four hundred miles in one day to see the American Indian monument that has already agreed to wait for us.") Then my mistake. "There's always tomorrow," I say.

He looks at me sternly, answers rapidly, vehemently. I hear anger I rarely hear from him. "That's not true. You can't count on tomorrow. Whoever said you could count on tomorrow? That's never a promise."

He opens the RV screen door, heads off for a walk. Returning, he is calmer. Sitting down in the small space, he agrees it might be good to stay an extra day, get refreshed for the road ahead. Lost time can be made up by reading a set of

Churchill's letters. "That's the other thing," he says, "I'm too old to read insignificant books—can't waste my eyesight hours on trash." He looks suspiciously at my stack of mysteries and romances.

DRIVING north, we head to Canada. We have seen photos of Alberta, but, as they say, no photo can do it justice. One evening we walk about a lake while a young man sits on the grass, strumming his guitar, entertaining a dozen mallards gathered on the water in front of him and his placid dog. We find a recommended restaurant where we dine on seafood stew—undoubtedly the best I have ever eaten, with crab and shrimp dancing in a pungent red sauce laced with clams and mussels and something indescribable. But in the middle of the night, I wake with a startle in the tiny RV bed, realizing my face and eyes are swelling, my throat sore and constricted. A victim of something indescribable.

I remain calm. "Rude, Rude, I hate to wake you, but I'm dying." Then, whispering to conserve my voice, I add, "I won't be able to talk much longer. Listen carefully. Get me to a hospital."

He uses only a moment to inspect me and the red rashes I have not yet seen, then he locates our shoes and jackets and we are off in the truck to find help. The campground night supervisor jots down directions to the emergency room. As it turns out, the doctor we need has just delivered a baby. He will finish up and meet us next door in his office.

The office door is unlocked and we sit alone in semi-darkness. When a portly, seventy-something man opens the door, a booming voice greets us. "My, my, let's get some lights on in here."

I assume the man is the receptionist until he throws a stethoscope around his neck. He glances at my closed eyes and twice-its-size face, takes my hand, and moves me rapidly down the short hallway toward an examining room. "Got to get to these problems fast—no time for pleasantries."

There is no time for the examining room either. We stand in the hallway, where he says, "I'm the nurse too. Drop those pajama bottoms, now, dearie. Let me at that bum." A rather long but virtually painless shot finds its way under the layers of skin and cellulite, and being a bit suggestible, I know the swelling is now receding like the Red Sea and I am healed. For good measure, the doctor hands me a package of Benadryl and his card. Rudy asks where the secretary is so that he might pay our bill. "I'm that too, the secretary," the doctor responds. "Let's see—I think that was worth about twenty dollars if you have it. Maybe fifteen. Just glad to be of help." Rudy hums "Oh Canada" all the way back to the campground.

In a few days I am, thanks to my personal Marcus Welby, rid of the last trace of rash and tiredness in time to join Rudy on a train trip. He loves trains and cannot sit for long within miles of a station without hopping aboard. He and the stationmaster work out an itinerary that involves only one night away from our fifth-wheel home. We will travel west to Kamloops, stay overnight there in a motel, then catch the early-morning train back to Jasper. It doesn't occur to me that these arrangements are a bit unusual for a train that goes across the country.

The train ride is beautiful if long, and we arrive at the darkened station at midnight to see only one taxi in the parking lot, its neon sign saying "Not Available." In minutes we learn that the taxi is unavailable because it waits for us. "The Jasper agent called ahead for you," the cab driver says, "so we're off to Kamloops' finest motel. I'm Bill. I called to be sure they saved that room for you. Can't have our guests sleeping out in the cold."

He drives us to a lovely lodge-style motel and helps us find registration cards and a room key behind the front desk. The manager is sleeping and there's no need to disturb him. "I'm so sorry not to be here to say good-bye in the morning," our driver says, "but I'm due on another route tomorrow. My friend Phil who drives the other cab will be here for you."

"I think the train leaves at six tomorrow," I say.

"Not a problem. Phil will take good care of you."

These acts of faith in strangers are hard for me and I barely sleep that night. Rudy snores happily. That morning, shortly before five o'clock, a soft knock wakes me. I struggle to find a robe, then open the door a bit. "I'm Phil," the man says. "Bill just called and said I should wake you up, since you might not have an alarm clock. He said to tell you he recommends we stop to pick up donuts—much better here in town than on the train. Do you want any coffee now?"

Canada turns out to be a hybrid travel destination, a place for slowing down but not stopping. It can be reached by driving through magnificent U.S. national parks, and is just different enough (think British heritage) to be interesting to my mate, just familiar enough to be comforting to me. I know how to find the emergency-room doctors.

AS time goes on, the erosion of the Rules continues. We meet forces even stronger than the lure of cruise ships and RVs— aging, illness, time itself. Even the fifth-wheeler slows down, parking now for much of the summer on a quiet, local lake-shore. Although Rudy no longer talks about his intention to camp in all fifty states, he has an urgency about his daily life.

He balks at my suggestion that he slow down, relax. His den is crowded with projects in progress—watercolor paint-ings on easels, the beginnings of a radio-controlled boat, a papier-mâché parrot waiting for its final coat, a computer packed with letters and advice to his congressmen. He and his daughter Day are on a waiting list for the Honor Flight, a trip to Washington D.C. to visit the World War II monu-ment. "I need to go now," he tells the organizers. "You never know about tomorrow."

One evening he gathers a half dozen fellow environmen-talists in our living room. They are planning their next anti-development demonstration when Rudy admits he feels chest pains. No, he will not go to the hospital up the street, but will instead call their emergency room to learn the approximate wait time.

"I don't have time to waste standing in your line," he tells the nurse. "We have an important cause we're working on here."

My spouse and I are not amateurs at this illness business. Shortly after our first trip together, Rudy contracted Guillain-Barré paralysis, a side effect of rolling up his sleeve for the new swine flu shot. School principals had been asked to model faith in the new immunization, and his near-deadly dose was administered on the school stage before a PTA audience. I came to the hospital each evening to read his favorite book, Steinbeck's *Travels with Charley*. He pushed himself through a year-long rehabilitation. He had to get back on the road.

Twenty years later, when Rudy's turn as caregiver came, he spread world maps across the floor of the medical center during my day-long chemo infusions, pulled out a clipboard and marking pens, and we began planning. Nurses stepped around the maps, taking time to point out their favorite destinations, and in some cases, to submit to Rudy's counseling services. Critical illness tried these times to interrupt our travel dreams, but travel dreams won, interrupting critical illness.

But this time, I am thinking, illness is joining forces with aging, and I know that is a combination we cannot beat. I see the changes in our family room. Foreign maps and "Let's Go" guidebooks that in the past were strung across the room are replaced first by tour and cruise brochures, then camp directories, trip insurance forms, and vacation rental photos. Criteria for destinations change from "adventurous" and "exotic" to "nearby" and "comfortable." For the first time, we seek familiar places, rentals where we know the reading chairs and lamps are good, where the walking paths are flat and the small grocery store is just around the corner. Where once we would inquire if the vacation rental was near mass transit, now we want to know if there is an elevator and if the walk-in shower has grab bars. I see the transitions on our packing lists. Cross off "walking boots," "walking stick," "day pack." Add "cane," "medicine chest," "sleep apnea machine," and eventually "walker," "portable oxygen," "wheelchair."

More than once we have said "last trip," but this last time I mean it. Two emergency room visits in a two-week vacation tell us it is time to stay home. Correction: they tell one of us.

Rudy, pushing his walker, finds me in the kitchen putting finishing touches on a cranberry salad. We are home for the Christmas holidays, after only briefly considering a fourteen-hour train trip to Seattle, where the family will celebrate brother Dick's eightieth birthday and niece Cindy's victory over the *Wheel of Fortune.* Rudy has been thinking.

"I have to go, Mare. I have to be part of this."

I voice concern. A lot of concern. He was released from the hospital just two weeks ago, after facing down another powerful attack of pneumonia. He had often said that travel was just too hard now. And the train route goes in high mountain altitude and he will need oxygen. What's more, the day after Christmas the train will be packed.

In the end, I find it impossible to argue with Rudy's own logic.

"But I'm so proud of Cindy," he says, "and Dick has always been there for me. I owe him. And I can see the whole family again, and . . ." The blue eyes are watery and fixed squarely on me. "Besides," he says, "it will be my last hurrah."

The next day, I am in Penney's menswear section at the mall, at the after-Christmas sale, buying the last warm scarf for Rudy to wear on his train trip, when my phone rings.

"Say there, pick me up a fedora-type hat, something brown to match my coat. No ball caps this trip. I'm changing my style to more gentlemanly, more dignified. Don't worry about the cost."

Who is this man? I say I will do what I can here at the end-of-season sale. As I make my promise, I turn around to the next nearly barren counter and there it sits all by itself—one brown plaid fedora-type dignified hat, price no object.

Two days later, at three a.m., on what has to be the coldest, darkest morning in recorded northern California history, the train sounds its arrival. It takes every able-bodied passenger in the Amtrak station to lift Rudy with his walker and oxygen tank and our luggage into the small compartment for the disabled. This time Rudy does not protest the label. His daughter Day and nephew Tom board this polar express at other stations, buoying up my courage.

And courage I need. That night there is a record-setting storm, one of the fiercest in years in the Cascade mountain range. As we approach one particularly daunting peak, the train slows more and more, coming at last to a complete stop. All we can see is white land, gray skies. Tom brings news that the train must wait here until a federal avalanche inspector arrives through the storm and approves our moving forward. One or two hours into our wait, I walk through the narrow corridors of the sleeper cars, reaching the dining area. I buy a bagful of snacks, favoring nutritious protein bars, then as nonchalantly as possible inquire about our future.

"And so, I suppose you have a lot of backup food, like enough for a lot of extra meals? I suppose these little layovers happen all the time and you're always prepared . . ."

I tell myself to relax and take those breaths, beat down those thoughts of the Donner Party.

We sit in the snow for seven more hours awaiting clearance to move. I try to find the user's manual for Rudy's oxygen tank. Is there enough oxygen for a snowstorm? Enough for an avalanche? There are grumbling, fearful, sometimes tearful passengers in all the compartments except one.

"These things happen in travel, Mare. Just look how beautiful the snow is. You should be enjoying it."

Slightly after three a.m., our train moves quietly into the deserted Seattle Amtrak station. There, struggling to stay awake in their cars, is our family. They have brought a wheelchair, and for once Rudy sits in it without protest.

"Do we dare ask how the trip was?" one niece ventures.

Rudy is the only one of us who replies, and his voice has vigor. "It was really great. I mean, we got here, didn't we? And you should have seen the snow."

Our three-day visit passes quickly, filled with the stuff of Seattle family reunions—stories, teasing, laughter, wine, mounds of fresh crab. Rudy is king, presiding over the crab and the wine and the stories. As we pack to go home, the family presents him with a black T-shirt with white lettering, a souvenir from Pike Place Market. He wastes no time putting it on.

"Life is not a journey to the grave with the intention of arriving safely, in a pretty and well-preserved body, but rather to skid in broadside, thoroughly used up, totally worn out, and loudly proclaiming '"WOW, what a ride!"'

TWO months after the train trip, in early spring, Rudy sits propped up in a hospital bed in the intensive-care unit, chairing a meeting about the end of his life. Somehow, the school principal persona is back.

"Is everybody comfortable in his chair?" he asks. "Who would like to start?"

The three doctors are clear: his body is shutting down, organs are failing, one by one, the pace quickening. Does he understand that, they want to know. He does, he says, but if there is any way they can get him two more years, he has five projects to complete. They leave the room shocked but not really surprised.

"He's a warrior," one says. "He'll never really give up."

Once we are alone, Rudy motions to me to shut the door and come closer, to put my ear to his mouth. He has that intent look I know so well. I recognize it even through the cloudiness of his now-soft blue eyes.

"I made a mistake. I should have asked for three years."

A week after Rudy (or Rudy's body) leaves us, I ask the counselor, "What do you think death is?"

"I think about it a lot," he says. "I think death might be a series of transitions or stages. At first it can seem that the loved one is very close, near at hand. Gradually that sense of closeness seems to fade for most people."

"And do you think stronger personalities are any different?"

He smiles, apparently remembering Rudy. "I've wondered about that, wondered if they seem present longer, if they exert influence longer. Why are you thinking about this today?"

"Because he's sitting in his favorite chair right now, but he never sat for long," I answer. "I just don't know what to expect next. I always like to be prepared."

CHAPTER TWENTY-TWO

TEN MONTHS AFTER THE TRAIN TRIP AND EIGHT MONTHS AFTER
Rudy dies, in early fall, I make a phone call to a tour agency. I
tell myself I can do this. I can travel a distance alone. I can
stop crying. I can stop crying if I just get out of this house.

It has been awhile since I have been through security at
an airport. I hand my boarding pass and driver's license to
the TSA agent, and she gives them a cursory look and says,
"You're on your own. It's up to you."

How does she know this? "I'm on my own. But what's up to me?" I ask.

She laughs loudly; apparently this is very funny. "No," she explains. "I was talking to that new agent standing behind you. You're not on your own."

"Oh, but I am," I say.

I do well for the first hour on the plane, burying myself in a South Dakota guidebook. I am, after all, on a family-roots trip, ready to see the land that seduced Grandfather with promises of gold and gambling, that sustained my parents until, after the Great Depression, it could no longer. I have traveled the world, but I have never spent time in South Dakota. In the quiet, my seat mate, a grandmotherly woman, looks at my wedding ring and asks, "So, are you alone? Your husband didn't come?"

"No," I say, "He couldn't make it this time."

There is much to recommend this tour. Flying over the Badlands, I find strange comfort: this destination mirrors the starkness, the stillness in me. My room at the lodge has a balcony looking directly across to the presidents of Mount Rushmore, who surely will share wisdom with me. My tour companions are well read and polite, and the excursions are interesting, almost interesting enough to distract me from the full-time occupation of grieving.

One evening, some of the group have seen a weather report that warns: "Put an extra blanket on. There may be a little drop in temperature." It was eighty-seven degrees earlier this week, so we are not afraid. It is barely October, after all.

The first hints of trouble are the absolute stillness of the morning and the absolute darkness of my room. In the five nights I have been at the lodge, cars outside have predictably awakened me by six o'clock, my nightlight offering a compass to the bathroom. This morning there is only quiet and darkness, and when I at last find the drapes, I open them to white—mounds and mounds of white, rising high above my windowpane, covering every surface, blocking any escape.

I curse my desire to have a quiet room, isolated far at the end of the lodge, with stone presidents my sole, mute companions. It is cold already without power for the electric heater. In the dark I struggle to find clothes, dress in all of them, layer upon layer, quickly realizing fall season tops and pants and tennis shoes are not cold-weather ready. My too-small flashlight is only slightly helpful, shining a narrow beam on merely one object at a time. Brushing my teeth involves focusing the beam first to find the brush, then back to locate paste, trying to remember where the brush is, connecting the two, finding molars. Once brushed and mummified, buried far down in the slightly warm bed, I wipe tears, waiting for the breakfast call, trying to imagine what Rudy would do. I get two pieces of advice from my meditation: "Cover your tennis shoes with something—even plastic bags maybe. Don't let them get wet. And remember your deep breathing."

My cell phone rings and rings, and in time I uncover it from beneath my bedding. My older brother has been following my search for "grandfather clues" from Deadwood to the Homestake mines, calling each day to see if there is anything more I have discovered. I know he really calls to be sure I am surviving my first trip alone. This morning he takes no time for light conversation. He spent much of his childhood in

South Dakota before our parents moved to California, and he remembers storms.

"I have the Weather Channel on. Tell me you're not still in the Black Hills."

I take a deep breath, giving it a try, but my voice wavers. "Okay, I'm not still in the Black Hills."

His voice is softer. "Tell me the truth this time. Where are you?"

"Still at the lodge in the Black Hills, near the National Park, with a whole tour group. We'll be fine."

"That's not what the Weather Channel says. And say, you still have electricity, don't you? You can't trust electricity in this kind of storm. How much charge do you have on that phone?"

In the deep, cold darkness, I check the cell phone battery. "Twenty percent. I must have forgotten to recharge it last night." Then I lie again. "I'll have to recharge it right away. I guess I'd better go now. Love you."

"Love you too. I won't call often. It's best to save that phone battery. You call when you need to."

"Right."

✈

I don't buy that ignorance is bliss, but I do agree it can be helpful. Our group does not know at first that we are stranded without a working generator on an impassable road, in an unseasonable blizzard with mounting seventy-mile-an-hour winds, a storm violent even by Dakota standards. One thing, however, is clear: if you are going to be captive for days in a record-breaking storm, be captive with the South Dakota

Rural Women in Agriculture. The women, here for a conference, stoke the lone large fireplace, help staff inventory supplies and plan food rationing, charge our cell phones in their
trucks, shovel relentless snow from walkways, and find board
games. We naïve non-ranchers realize only gradually that
while the women support us, their cattle at home freeze in
ice-covered fields.

Two days into the storm, our luck changes. A catering
truck is stranded in a snow bank while it tries to deliver a
wedding feast to the lodge. The driver stumbles through
mounds of snow only to learn the wedding has been cancelled. No guests could possibly reach the destination, so the
bounty is ours: shrimp, stuffed salmon, tri-tip, twice-baked
potatoes, wines, and the most delicious cake any of us have
ever eaten. Someone carefully lifts the bride and groom fig-
ures from atop the cake and wraps them in tissue for the next
wedding date.

I am tolerating the days of card games and fireside
companionship, but the dark, cold nights only get harder,
lonelier. Almost everyone is traveling with a spouse. At
night I am on my own, just as the TSA woman said. These
strangers, my tour mates, seem to know my coping skills are
marginal, getting frayed. They watch me rather intently.
They must wonder what possessed me to take this trip so
soon. So soon after. I wonder too.

At noon on the next day of captivity, as blue sky emerges
above white, we have word that the road seems clear enough
for well-equipped jeeps to try to reach Rapid City, the town
below. A bus will "likely" come tomorrow for the rest of the
group. There is one seat left in the Cherokee that will leave

in five minutes. I do not like the word "try" as in "try to reach the town," but I don't much like the word "likely" about the chance of a bus coming tomorrow. I have an association with Rapid City: my parents, who had lived in a miniscule town, spoke of the city as Mecca. Perhaps it will be for me too. At the very least, it has an airport. More to the point, I am not sure I can face one more night here. But leave in five minutes? I have never made a decision in five minutes. As it turns out, I don't have to make a decision—it is made for me by my new friends, who say, "You know you have to get out of here."

There is the matter of packing. Three of my card-playing buddies rush with me to my room and throw everything in the suitcase, then find my jacket, give me gloves and a hat, and I am on my way. The trip down the mountain takes a skilled, calm driver and we have one. The beauty of the ride fades as we see cows and calves lying frozen in fields, cars on both sides of the road fallen into ditches, barns collapsed. Later we learned that at least 75,000 cows had perished in five feet of snow.

As we come into Rapid City, we notice there are no signs of power in homes or on the streets. The hotel we approach has dim lighting, perhaps from a generator. More importantly, one room is left, for me. I hear the catch in my voice as I thank our driver, say good-bye, and realize I am alone again. The desk clerk assures me I can stay until the airport reopens. The airport has been heavily damaged, so my dream of flying home tomorrow flies away.

"You know, it's just too bad you couldn't have been here with us last night," the clerk says. "The Red Hat ladies are here for a convention. The jazz band they hired got stranded on the Interstate. Then the town's Oktoberfest had to be cancelled. So the jazz band never showed up, but the oompahpah band came here and played polkas all night. It was a great night, people polkaing everywhere. You would have loved it. You're from these parts, aren't you?"

I think of my roots. "Yes, yes, I think you could say I am. I've just been gone a long time."

The laundry is open, she says, the coffee shop has some food left, and I am in time to attend a wedding, if I wouldn't mind helping two kids whose family and bridal party are stranded on Interstate 90. He is in the military and has to report to base; they can't wait for their guests to dig out from the snow banks.

"You don't happen to be a minister, do you?" she asks. "A lot of people carry those little cards that let them be ministers."

I shake my head.

I stop in my room before the ceremony is due to begin. This room has luxuries—a television, a heater, a shower with hot water, lamps, and electricity to charge my cell phone. After a very quick wash, I head downstairs where a Red Hat lady escorts me to a seat in the coffee shop that doubles now as a chapel. Group singing begins as the bride enters: "Love, look at the two of us . . ." I needn't have worried about the state of my outfit, as the bride and groom's wedding clothing is stranded on the Interstate along with the family. The couple is in jeans and plaid shirts. To add a touch of dignity, the Red Hat lady volunteering as matron of honor removes her hat and places it on the bride. At the end of the short, sweet ceremony, another takes off her own hat and passes it through the misty-eyed audience.

In the coffee shop day and night I find people to talk to. I am feeling at home in this place. Everyone has a storm story to tell. One local woman is interested in genealogy and in my pre-storm search for family in the hills of South Dakota and Czechoslovakia. I carry three small photos taken in the 1920s, two of my parents, one of our Bohemian grandfather. It is the photo of Grandfather that catches her eye.

"Have you noticed his complexion is darker than the others? His eyes are large and very dark too. Have you noticed his elegant jacket and bow tie?"

"No, I haven't seen all that, but, yes, I see it now that you point it out."

"I shouldn't say just from this photo, but if you're researching this man and your lineage, dear, you might want to read about the gypsies of Bohemia."

The gypsies of Bohemia? My lineage? I try to tell her I am not our family gypsy. He died.

"My husband was half Hungarian. A lot of gypsies are Hungarian, aren't they?"

She smiles at me. "Well, yes, but a lot of gypsies are Bohemian."

The next morning the skies are even bluer but the roadways are narrow, icy, slippery. I tell the desk clerk, "I didn't expect the storm or imagine that the airport would be shut down so long. I didn't bring enough medicine for an extra week. I'm usually very careful in my packing, but this time, well, I had some problems . . ."

"Easy," she says. "The hotel driver will take you in our

van to the pharmacy. It'll be an exciting ride maybe, but the snow is really beautiful."

I have heard those words before, on a train ride. I ask the driver if I can sit up front. I want to see it all.

LATE that night, I sit in a corner of the coffee shop, revising my Rules again. I add, "bring really large flashlight, extra meds, emergency charger . . ." and a rule from Rudy: "'Relax. Kind strangers will appear.'"

Mary's Rules
for
Travel

1. **REMAIN ALERT. ALWAYS.**

2. **EXPECT THE WORST.**

   Pack door locks, emergency charger, antibiotic wipes, insect repellent, large flashlights, protein bars, face masks, toilet seat covers, water purifier, mosquito netting, emergency phone numbers for doctors, bankers, the U.S. embassy.

3. **THERE IS NO SUCH THING AS A FREE LUNCH. (AND) YOU GET WHAT YOU PAY FOR.**

   There is a reason that hotel has the best price and the café a seafood special.

4. **IN PARTICULAR, DO NOT SKIMP ON TRANSPORTATION.**

   There is no National Transportation Safety Board where you are going. Unobtrusively, inspect tires on buses, vans, and rickshaws. If you can find a casual way to bring this up, ask how the brakes are doing.

5. **PREPARE FOR MEDICAL EMERGENCIES.**

   Pack a case of prescription and over-the-counter remedies for any ailment you have had in the last five years, as well as for any disease you know to be hereditary. Add megadose vitamins, antibiotics, rescue inhaler, GI-tract remedies for either extreme, bandages, knee and ankle braces. Purchase evacuation insurance.

6. **PREPARE FOR THEFT.**
   Carry a list of credit card numbers, leaving out segments of the numbers in case that list is stolen. Leave another copy with a family member at home, unless that member causes concern.

7. **RELAX. KIND STRANGERS WILL APPEAR.**

Epilogue

Rudy's Rule 14:
DON'T LET DEATH KEEP YOU
FROM TRAVELING

TODAY I WILL GO TO A FUNERAL, THE FIRST SINCE RUDY'S
death several months ago. I will honor Alta Mae, one of his
cherished colleagues. I put on a fitted black jacket and look
in the hall mirror. My staring, reddened eyes say it all: I am
in no shape to go anywhere, let alone a funeral. There will
not be enough Kleenex.

Slipping off the jacket and kicking off my shoes, I head to the laundry room. In the months since Rudy died, washing towels has been a central part of my day. I know just how much detergent to add, in which cycle, then just how long to set the dryer. There is hardly anything else I have mastered since his death.

The decision is easy now. I must stay home because I have to watch the laundry. Changed into sweat pants and shirt, I go to gather the mail. Apparently I have not been at my box for many days. Amidst the tangled, tall stack of envelopes and catalogs, a letter from the Salvation Army gets my attention. It must not be another solicitation; it is addressed to me by hand. Inside is a letter of apology.

> *We sincerely regret the delay in this notification. Several weeks ago, a donor, Alta Mae Talbot, made a very generous gift to us in loving memory of your husband, Rudy Jensen. We apologize for not notifying you in a timely manner. Please accept our sincere condolences.*

The funeral is half over when I arrive, but friends wave and point to the seat they have saved for me. I have a few words with Rudy before I move toward the mourners.

"I admit I needed a bit of a nudge, but you—you've got to be less controlling now that you're gone."

MONTHS later, I tell the counselor, "I'm not the type, not the type to claim visions or form friendships with ghosts. I don't read books about the paranormal or go to séances. I'm what you would call a 'skeptic.' You'll notice that my eyebrows are in a semi-permanent raised position.

"Yes, things have changed a bit over time, just as you said they might. He's not so much involved in life at the house any more . . . but I have to tell you, he seems to have begun traveling again."

✈

THE small commuter plane linking California's central valley to San Francisco is supposed to fly me away from my memories. Instead it reminds me of flights around the globe. I want to ask Rudy if he, too, sees the resemblance between this pilot and one in the Costa Rica jungle who, once up in the air, explained why our four-passenger craft needed to return to base. ("Down, down, plane down.") We got it. Free drinks in the bar he conveniently owned helped pass the time while we watched him replace three parts.

Today I have the aisle seat I want, one close to the front for easy escape. (Smaller planes are known to have higher crash rates.) The window seat next to me stays vacant. I start to spread out my carry-on bags when I realize that the cabin door is being reopened and more passengers boarded. I don't bother to condense my belongings—there are plenty of free spaces. But a tall, thin young man stops, sees the empty seat, rechecks his ticket.

He looks at me and says softly, "I belong with you."

He must have seen me startle—that was a familiar phrase in our house. Recovering, I gather my carry-ons and stand to let him take the window seat. He takes off a heavy jacket to reveal his pullover sweater is white, emblazoned with the green and yellow University of Oregon emblem. Rudy's school, his team.

I need more information. "So, you're a student at the university in Eugene?"

"I am. Do you know that school? Not many Californians do."

"Yes, I know it well. My husband and I lived there for several years while I was in grad school, some time ago. But he died."

"Oh, I'm sorry. I don't know what to say."

He is young; he thinks he must say something.

"Did he just love the place? It's only my first year but already I do."

"He most loved the environment, the natural beauty everywhere—and the Ducks football. He even loved the rain."

"That's funny, that's just what I love."

I am taking the early-morning train home from San Jose. Escaping the crowded Amtrak lobby, I find the track, but I must be early. A young man and I are alone in the darkness, on the benches. For a long time, he looks down, but when finally he raises his head and looks at me, he and his blue eyes are familiar. So is his Oregon Duck shirt. There are nine hundred seats on this commuter train, and he sits opposite me. He does not talk, just sits and reads an American history text.

THE day before my niece Diane and I are to begin a road trip north to Seattle for a wedding, the manager at the cemetery calls me. The headstone for Rudy's grave has arrived and been placed. They would like me to see it, so we arrange to spend time there on our way home.

I had struggled for weeks over the wording of the stone. How could I describe this force in twenty characters? I had settled on "Beloved, Kind Warrior."

I know how impatient Rudy can get. As we approach the freeway exit to the cemetery, I roll down our windows and call to him.

"We'll be back, honey. We're on our way to Emily's wedding. We'll have lots of time when—"

Diane's scream interrupts my sentence. "Look, look to the right."

There is either a mirage or a large, shiny new green and yellow carrier truck in the next lane, pulling ahead of us, the Duck mascot emblazoned on all sides of the University of Oregon vehicle, here, hundreds of miles from its campus.

Diane readies her camera and shouts directions. "Nobody's going to believe us. Pick up speed and pass the truck. Pull off at the first exit and I'll jump out and get the picture."

It takes time for a mirage to appear. We stand a long time in the midst of an offramp up the road, camera at the ready, and no Duck truck in sight. Just when we begin to believe we have had some sort of shared hallucination, the truck appears on the highway next to us, its driver looking confused when we wave, scream, and take his picture.

The wedding venue in Seattle is beautiful. A newly restored hotel down the street houses the whole family, and when Diane and I arrive we have a warm welcome, our younger nieces and nephews showing us to our rooms. In my room, I notice they exchange whispers and look a little anxious.

When I open the room's heavy drapes, I understand. Across the narrow street is a barber shop with a large neon sign facing directly into my bedroom.

"Rudy's," it says.

AT home, I postpone cleaning his closet as long as I can. As winter weather approaches again, I try not to notice his warm coats, jackets, fur hat. Someone needs these things, I finally tell myself, and if I listen carefully another voice says it is time. A friend and I bundle the clothes: in each stack, garments in yellow and green form an entire wardrobe of tribute to the University of Oregon Ducks football team.

Shelter residents help me unload my car trunk, thanking me over and over for warmth. This winter when I walk downtown, I startle each time I come face to face with a familiar Oregon Ducks vest or sweater. One homeless man in yellow and green camps in front of my favorite store, greets me like he knows me. We exchange our anthem: "Go Ducks."

I need to talk to that counselor again. It has been nearly four years since Rudy died and he is still testing the theory that time will fade the intensity of his presence. I admit, though, that he has been more quiet lately—no dramatic coincidences, no sense he has something to say or anyplace to go—until this week.

My family gathers in Seattle, staying in a venerable bed and breakfast west of the city. It is rare that we can all be in one place at one time and we are relishing that. As we walk into the inn to register, a recording of Louis Armstrong proclaims "It's a Wonderful World," a Rudy-favorite tune that was the theme at his memorial. One niece reminds us that we have not all been together since that memorial.

"Uncle Rudy would have loved this reunion," she says. "Think of all he went through on the train to get to his last party here."

I wonder to myself if that party here four years ago was really Rudy's last. I can't imagine him ever having a *last* party.

✈

A celebration is planned for tonight. It is my brother's birthday. It was my brother's birthday that four years ago brought Rudy to Seattle on his triumphant train ride through avalanche country.

Now, in keeping with family tradition, it is time for naps before the party. Each of the room doors closes quietly. I go to my room, kick off my shoes, climb into the high bed, and place my iPhone on the pillow next to me as I always do. But this time, as I set it down it blasts music. I have never used my phone for music; I come from the generation that says phones are for making and receiving phone calls. I have never even spoken to Siri. Yet here at this family reunion, the phone chooses "Hail, Hail, the Gang's All Here" and it chooses to play it louder and louder and louder.

The bedroom doors open and my nieces follow the blaring, blasting sounds to my room. I have been unable to turn the music off or even down. My hands are shaking and that is part of the problem, but it seems not to be the whole explanation, for even our tech guru Cindy labors to control the sound. Finally, the phone submits, quiets, but when she looks at the screen he announces himself.

"From Rudy Jensen's iPod Playlist," it says.

It takes awhile for hearts to settle down to normal rhythms, and hands to stop shaking, but just as we calm, the phone begins to play Mozart's *"Eine Kleine Nachtmusik"* ("A Little Night Music"), Rudy's favorite classical piece. Just to be sure she has identified the messenger, Cindy turns the phone over and reads once again on the screen: "From Rudy Jensen's iPod Playlist."

Somehow she quiets the phone, is able to turn it off, and this time it stays quiet. Messages received. She attempts a theory about how Rudy's playlist from four years ago could have migrated now from his small computer to his Cloud, then jumped somehow onto my Cloud, but she has no explanation for the musical choice, the perfectly timed message, nor the independence of a time traveler who never misses a Seattle party.

I am just pleased to know he has made it to The Cloud. Wherever that is.

SOMETIMES I understand things by knowing what they are not. I am in the audience when Poet Laureate Robert Pinsky reads "An Old Man." The old man is not Rudy. He is definitely not Rudy.

AN OLD MAN

After Cavafy

Back in a corner, alone in the clatter and babble
An old man sits with his head bent over a table
And his newspaper in front of him, in the café.

Sour with old age, he ponders a dreary truth—
How little he enjoyed the years when he had youth,
Good looks and strength and clever things to say.

He knows he's quite old now: he feels it, he sees it,
And yet the time when he was young seems—was it?
Yesterday. How quickly, how quickly it slipped away.

Now he sees how Discretion has betrayed him,
And how stupidly he let the liar persuade him
With phrases: *Tomorrow. There's plenty of time. Some day.*

He recalls the pull of impulses he suppressed,
The joy he sacrificed. Every chance he lost
Ridicules his brainless prudence a different way.

But all these thoughts and memories have made
The old man dizzy. He falls asleep, his head
Resting on the table in the noisy café.

ACKNOWLEDGMENTS

After Rudy's death, *Tales and Memories*, his account of his young years, sat on my bookshelf, trying its best to move me to action. I had promised him I would someday add the story of our marriage and our journeys, but for a time illness and grieving were not compatible with writing. My Irish mother taught me the value of superstition, and I developed a mighty one that said, "If only I am in a structured writing class, I will be structured. I will write."

I came early one fall day to register at Chico State's Osher Lifelong Learning Institute, only to learn that the writing class was already filled by people who obviously didn't need its structure as much as I did. I approached the instructor, Jim Smith, just as Martha Roggli, a woman I had never seen before and whose name I knew only from her name tag, took my arm and pleaded with him. "This is my dear, dear friend (she looks at my name tag)—Mary—and we both have to have this class. We have major projects underway. You'll need to open a new section."

I have a major project underway? Two classes a week for Jim?

"Wait till you see how well behaved we'll be," Martha insists. And Jim, warm-hearted soul, capitulates.

I owe Jim and Martha for the gifts of structure and faith, and each of our Wednesday Morning Writers for their faithful editing and loving encouragement. I thank Rudy for leaving his words and Cheri Taylor for steady, calm technical support.

I am grateful for She Writes Press, particularly Brooke Warner, Cait Levin, and Stacey Aaronson who so generously shared their expertise and inspiration.

My friends and family have been tireless in encouraging me. They were my anchors.

I owe you all so much.

$\mathcal{A}$BOUT THE $\mathcal{A}$UTHOR

MARY K. JENSEN is a recovering grants writer and professor who, in her retirement from California State University, Chico, ventured into her attic and pulled out boxes of trip diaries, raw material for her memoir, *Rudy's Rules for Travel*. Mary is a survivor, of cancer two times, and of decades of travel with her risk-taking spouse. She earned her Ph.D. at the University of Oregon where she was an analyst and writer for a federal research clearinghouse. Prior to her doctoral training, she worked in California schools, in an array of roles: teaching, school psychology, and administration. She co-authored numerous educational studies and the text, *Games Children Should Play: Sequential Lessons for Teaching Communication*. She is a member of California Writers Club and is published in North State Writers' 2017 anthology. Mary lives now in northern California where she relishes her writing class, book clubs, poetry group, walks, and friend-ships.

Visit Mary at www.marykjensen.com

SELECTED TITLES FROM SHE WRITES PRESS

She Writes Press is an independent publishing company
founded to serve women writers everywhere.
Visit us at www.shewritespress.com.

Gap Year Girl by Marianne Bohr. $16.95, 978-1-63152-820-0.
Thirty-plus years after first backpacking through Europe, Marianne
Bohr and her husband leave their lives behind and take off on a
yearlong quest for adventure.

*Peanut Butter and Naan: Stories of an American Mother in The Far
East* by Jennifer Magnuson. $16.95, 978-1-63152-911-5. The hi-
larious tale of what happened when Jennifer Magnuson moved her
family of seven from Nashville to India in an effort to shake things
up—and got more than she bargained for.

This is Mexico: Tales of Culture and Other Complications by Carol M.
Merchasin. $16.95, 978-1-63152-962-7. Merchasin chronicles her
attempts to understand Mexico, her adopted country, through im-
probable situations and small moments that keep the reader moving
between laughter and tears.

*Flip-Flops After Fifty: And Other Thoughts on Aging I Remembered to
Write Down* by Cindy Eastman. $16.95, 978-1-938314-68-1. A
collection of frank and funny essays about turning fifty—and all
the emotional ups and downs that come with it.

Renewable: One Woman's Search for Simplicity, Faithfulness, and Hope
by Eileen Flanagan. $16.95, 978-1-63152-968-9. At age forty-
nine, Eileen Flanagan had an aching feeling that she wasn't living
up to her youthful ideals or potential, so she started trying to
change the world—and in doing so, she found the courage to
change her life.

Dearest Ones at Home: Clara Taylor's Letters from Russia, 1917-1919
edited by Katrina Maloney and Patricia Maloney. Clara Taylor's
detailed, delightful letters documenting her two years in Russia
teaching factory girls self-sufficiency skills—right in the middle of
World War I.